How To Understand Federal Government Solicitations and Win Government Contracts

A proven guide to maximize your win probability,
and save time, resources, and B&P budget

By Rob Ransone

Rob Ransone
415 Fearrington Post
Pittsboro, NC 27312
919.533.6923
ransone@aol.com

www.ransone.com

How To
Understand Federal Government Solicitations
and
Win Government Contracts

A proven guide to maximize your win probability
and save time, resources, and B&P budget

Overview and Introduction

This book is based upon experiences acquired during more than 50 years on both sides of the Federal Government product and services solicitations business. The information and ideas presented here have been informally reviewed and discussed with representatives of industry, Government, and academia.

Throughout this book you will see the designation "solicitation." This encompasses Request for Information (RFI), Request for Proposals (RFP), Request for Quotations (RFQ), and Broad Area Announcements (BAA). Any differences are addressed on a case-by-case basis. Throughout this book I use the word "response" instead of "proposal" to include all submissions in response to all types of government solicitations.

You will see occasional references to "AWWS." This refers to the Advanced Widget Warning System, a fictitious RFP for an automobile radar warning receiver, used for proposal training.

The following summary describes what you will learn in each section. You may chose to read straight through, or just read or review specific sections as you need.

Part I – Government Solicitations

In this section you will learn how the Government identifies, plans, organizes, and solicits offers, evaluates responses, and selects contractors for new products and services. You will also learn how the Government's concern for risk affects your evaluation so that you can address these concerns in your responses. If you are responding to a US Army solicitation you must also address the seven tenets of MANPRINT. Finally, you will learn what the Source Selection Authority (SSA), the single individual who makes the final selection for contract award, sees to make his or her decision, and how he or she makes that decision. The SSA is human, and, in spite of how carefully you construct your response, you must convince the SSA to choose you over all of your competitors—even those who may offer a lower price. You must convince the SSA that your offering guarantees less risk to his or her career, and provide enough information for the SSA to justify selecting you to the losing bidders' Congressman.

Part II – Analyzing Government Solicitations

In this section you will learn about the various parts of a Government solicitation, which ones you must follow explicitly, and which you can safely address in your own way. You will learn how to analyze Government solicitations to be 100% compliant with format requirements and 100% responsive to program requirements.

Part III – Win Strategies and Win Themes Development

In this section you will learn how to develop effective win strategies and themes that communicate your discriminators, and maximize your win probability. You will learn how to analyze the opportunity, your customer, your competitors, and yourself in order to determine whether you have a chance of winning a contract, or whether you would be wasting your time and money and should wait for a more winnable opportunity.

Part IV – Organizing your Response Team and Planning Your Response

In this section you will learn how to organize your response team and your response to be most effective and most efficient. You will learn how to work with your potential customer before the solicitation is released, how to budget your response to get the most "bang for the buck," and the practices and methods of successful bidders. Especially, you will learn what *not* to do, which would guarantee losing the opportunity.

Part V – Managing Your Response

In this section you will learn how to manage your response to save time and Bid & Proposal (B&P) money. You will learn the responsibilities of the various members of your team that can help to ensure an efficient and effective result. "Effectiveness" is doing the right thing. "Efficiency" is doing something the best way possible. It's a waste of resources to do something efficiently if it's not the right thing to do!

Part VI – Writing Winning Sales Documents

In this section you will learn how to convince the Government to choose you over all others—even those with a lower price. You will learn how to provide a response that is clear and concise and favored by evaluators, and how to avoid things that offend them. You will also learn how to prepare and present oral responses.

Part VII – Risk Assessment and Mitigation

In this section you will learn why your Risk Management Plan is so important to your customer, and how to prepare one that convinces your customer that his or her career is safer with your offering that with your competitors.

Part VII – Integrated Program Management (IPM)

In this section you will learn why the Integrated Master Plan (IMP) and Integrated Master Schedule (IMS) are important and how to prepare them with a common numbering scheme that tracks directly to your Contract Work Breakdown Structure (CWBS) and Contract Statement of Work (CSOW).

Part IX – Response Reviews and the End Game

In this section you will learn how to benefit from your last chance to "get it right" by planning and conducting effective reviews, and how to avoid last minute goofs during final revision, formatting, printing, and submitting.

Part X – Post Submission Actions

In this section you will learn what you can do after you submit your response that will help to save B&P money and improve your win probability on future opportunities.

Additional Reading

I have documented 50 years of proposals successes and failures in my book of case histories *So You Want To Be A Proposals Professional*.

PART I – GOVERNMENT SOLICITATIONS

How Government Prepares its Solicitations for
Products and Services and Evaluates Responses

How Government Buys New Products and Services

Bottom-up requirements definition–Mission Needs Statement (MNS), System Operational Requirements (SOR): Commonly, using commands identify products or services that they need through a Mission Needs Statement (MNS) or a System Operational Requirement (SOR). This request is submitted up the line for approval, and a Source Selection agency is appointed. That agency identifies the appropriate type of solicitation, and specialists define the details. Lawyers review the legal aspects and identify Congressional requirements and conditions. The entire solicitation development, preparation, and approval process is as complicated as you might expect Government bureaucracies to devise—no, even more so!

Solicitation announcements are multi-step actions that may include early public announcements of future needs, comments from industry, and revisions of requirements.

Solicitation announcements—Sources Sought: Once the need is verified, the agency's Contracting Office issues an invitation for potential bidders to identify themselves and their qualifications by a notice in the government FedBizOpps (FBO) database (Fed Biz Ops, FedBizOps, Fed Biz Opps), formerly known as the Commerce Business Daily (CBD), FedBizOps is the source for federal procurement bidding opportunities, contracts awarded, special notices, and surplus government sales. You can search using keywords/phrases relevant to your business or select from over 100 business categories using the FBO Online search engine service. You can also register and identify your interests in specific solicitations here, and identify other potential bidders for possible teaming, subcontracting, or other collaboration arrangements.

Getting solicitations approved–competitive bids or sole source: Once the Contracting Office receives responses to its notice in FedBizOps, and determines that there are potential interested bidders, the next big decision must be made: sole source procurement or competitive bidding. The Contracting Office must be convinced that strong, convincing factors support a sole source solicitation, or it must pursue a competitive bid. Sole source justification must be based upon conclusive evidence that one and only one company can provide the needed product or service and meet the operational and delivery schedule requirements. This justification must be strong enough that it will convince the disqualified bidders' congress people. Whether the acquisition will be competitive or sole source, the Contracting Office must determine the military sensitivity of the product or service. It may be full and open competition, including open for bids from friendly foreign companies; it may be limited to NO-FORN, which limits it to only US companies; it may be classified SECRET, which means that its disclosure could embarrass the US; it may be classified TOP SECRET, which means that its disclosure could lead to war; or it might even be classified BLACK-LIMITED ACCESS REQURED, which is so sensitive that only those with specific NEED TO KNOW can even be made aware of the program. Stealth technology is a typical example of the latter case. If the solicitation is classified, then only companies with facility clearances to that level are allowed access to the information. Sometimes only parts of a solicitation might be classified.

Requests for Information–RFI: Sometimes the needed product or service is so new that the Contracting Office does not have the necessary information to specify exactly what it needs in detail, and needs to find out from industry the available state-of-the-art. If this is the case, it issues a Request for Information (RFI) which asks potential bidders for their information pertaining to the solicited product or service.

Requests for Quotation–RFQ: If the need is simple, such as off-the-shelf supplies or services, the Contracting Office may issue a simple RFQ, which simply identifies what is needed, when it can be delivered, and how much it will cost. The Contracting Office then awards a contract to the bidder it believes offers the best "bang for the buck."

Requests for Proposals–RFP: If the need is complex and more than one bid is desired in order to benefit from competitive pricing, the Contracting Office issues an RFP. This is an extensive, expensive, time-consuming activity for which the Federal Acquisition Regulations (FAR) for commercial and Defense Federal Acquisition Regulation System (DFARS) for military solicitations, specify detailed, complex, and laborious processes that absolutely must be followed! Failure to follow any one of these detailed instructions can result in bidders' protests and Contracting Officer disciplinary actions. This is government complexity "in spades!" A competitive solicitation opens the opportunity to qualified bidders, and establishes the evaluation and decision process. More on this later.

Broad Agency Announcements BAA: Some Government agencies, notably those not in DoD, use the BAA process for soliciting products or services. Although the formats of these solicitations differ from that of RFPs, and the response formats are different, the basic response *process* is the same.

Unsolicited Proposals: Suppose you have a terrific idea and want to sell it to the government. This is an opportunity for an Unsolicited Proposal. The procedure for following your dream in this manner is substantially different from responding to government solicitations, since these are basically sole source, and are difficult for the Government to approve.

The Solicitation Schedule-DSARC

The Defense Systems Acquisition Review Council (DSARC) process establishes specific timelines and milestone "gates" through which a new product must pass in order to continue into operational use. The government's funding profile is keyed to this Milestone schedule, and your program must pass these government reviews in order to be allowed to continue into the next development or production phase.

Years ago using commands defined their needs in specific terms such as (for instance) a new anti-tank cannon. This resulted in a solicitation for an improved cannon, but that's all it did. It was discovered that by specifying the need so specifically, it limited the new item and did not benefit from new technology. This was changed so that the potential user defined only *what* the new item was needed to do, and left the *how* it was to be done up to industry innovations. Now the MENS states requirements such as: "We need a new way to kill tanks and armored vehicles." The procurement could then result in shoulder-mounted missiles, high-energy lasers, small air-to-ground missiles launched from helicopters, or unmanned aerial vehicles (UAVs). In order to improve this system the US Office of Management and Budget (OMB) issued Circular A-109. Its purpose is to express needs and program objectives in mission terms, and not equipment terms, in order to encourage innovation and competition in creating, exploring, and developing alternative system design concepts. This task precedes the DSARC acquisition schedule, and is sometimes referred to as Milestone 0 (zero).

The DSARC schedule is shown in the following figure:

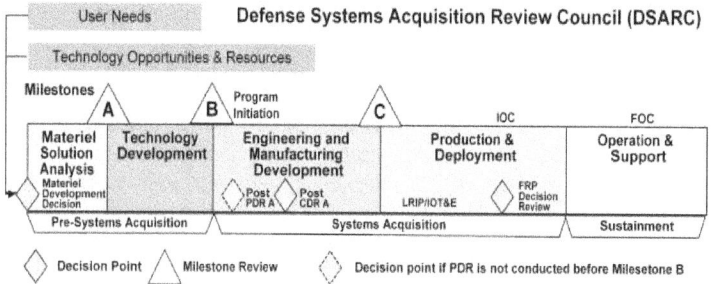

Milestone A is the start of the Demonstration and Validation phase. This period marks the beginning of the period where the Contractor and the System Program Office (SPO) prepare designs and conduct hardware testing. It can include wind tunnel tests, or other demonstrations that validate the technical approach. The program can continue only after the product has met all of the requirements of that phase. Sometimes the government makes multiple awards at this phase in order to define the best possible product or service.

Milestone B is the beginning of full scale development. This begins the phase where full scale hardware is developed, an initial batch of units is fabricated and tested, and production tooling is installed.

Milestone C is the approval to start production and delivery of the first operationally configured articles. A small quantity of these articles (Limited Rate Initial Production-LRIP) are delivered to the using command for operational testing and an Initial Operational Capability (IOC). This is where any operational problems are identified and corrected before the program can continue into Full Rate Production (FRP) and Full Operational Capability (FOC).

When you develop your response schedule, you absolutely *must* meet these government milestone dates, and provide the information the government needs to complete its DSARC Reviews.

Business Opportunities Announcement

The Government used to announce business opportunities through the Commerce and Business Daily (CBD), but now announces them through its website: https://www.fbo.gov/. At this website you can search for pending business opportunities from all government agencies, commercial vendors, and government buyers are invited to post, search, monitor, and retrieve opportunities solicited by the entire Federal contracting community. You can register your company or yourself on this web site, post your interest in specific opportunities, see who is considering responding to each solicitation, offer your services to other companies, track solicitation progress, download specific files and documents, and have the government notify you of specific solicitation activities of your interests. This is a terrific web site for anyone interested in government contracting.

When you access the web site, you are greeted with this home page:

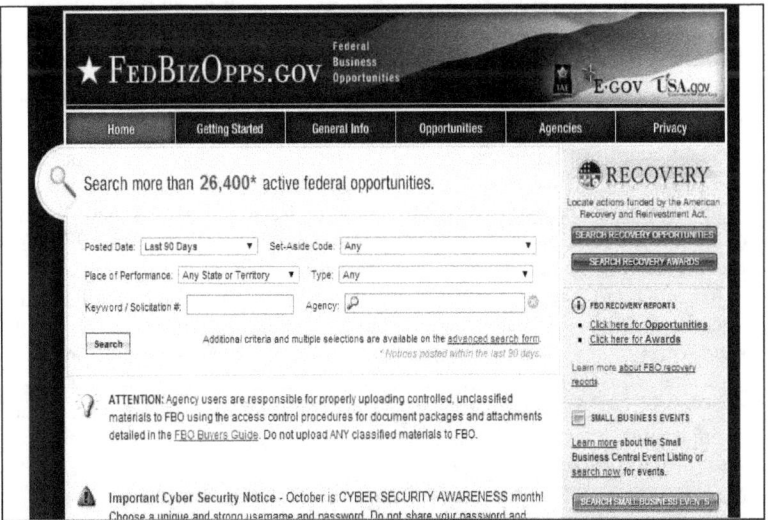

This web site is user friendly, and you should have no trouble navigating the sub screens. Once you register, when you find an opportunity that interests you, you only need to click on a button to insert your contact information as an interested vendor.

Sources Sought

Sometimes the Government will ask industry to justify its qualifications for specific opportunities through a Sources Sought announcement. For this response, you will state your technical and management capabilities relative to the specific job in order to be placed on the approved list to receive future specific solicitations.

Industry Day

When it is held: In order for industry to plan for and invest in a program it has to know the Government's plans in advance. The Government can use an Industry Day to meet with industry and ultimate end users of the service or product when developing the Performance Work Statement (PWS). This allows industry input in the process as soon as possible. An Industry Day may be held any time, either before or after a solicitation has been released.

How it is held: The government may conduct either a formal or an informal meeting. It usually presents a slide presentation and provides handouts. This may be more of a means of documenting what they divulged than a convenience to industry. It might or might not allow questions from industry.

War Story:
On one such meeting I had noticed there was no notice barring recording devices, so right at the outset of the meeting I held up mine, announced that I had seen no prohibition, and asked if it would be OK. The government hosts looked at each other in surprise, and said it would be OK. The rest of the industry attendees just glared at me!

What the Government expects: The Government will expect to learn what is available with respect to the state-of-the-art, industry capabilities, what it can reasonably expect to obtain, how long it will take, and how much to budget.

What you can expect: You can expect to learn of specific new business opportunities, identify your competitors and possible teaming relationships. You might even learn something of your competitors' ideas.

What to do and what not to do: Be careful of what you divulge. It will be a fine line between what you want to say to impress the Customer, and what you want to keep secret from your competitors. Be alert to what your competitors are saying or asking—this might divulge their approach or win strategy. Also, watch for competitors talking with each other because this can identify potential teaming arrangements.

Government Evaluation Process

You absolutely must understand how the Federal government accepts responses and evaluates them in order to avoid critical mistakes that can prevent the evaluators from even *seeing* your response.

Federal Acquisition Regulations (FAR) and Defense Federal Acquisition Regulations System (DFARS): The FAR is the rule book for non defense solicitations, and the DFARS is the rule book for defense related solicitations. These are *not guidelines*—they are the congressional mandates, the laws, which the federal government *must follow precisely* in order to level the playing field, and avoid discriminatory bias and grounds for industry protests.

Additional process rules for defense contracting: In addition to the FAR and DFARS, there are many individual directives in the 5000 series that have additional requirements for all levels of federal government solicitations.

Solicitation Section M Evaluation Factors versus the Source Selection Plan (SSP): The Government provides "hints" in Section M, Evaluation Factors for Award, of *what* it will evaluate and *how it will score* your response, but the government *does not* actually evaluate your response in accordance with these factors.. The real evaluation and scoring process is provided to its evaluators in the official SSP, to which you don't have access, because these are basically the "answer sheets" for scoring your response. The FARs prohibit the government from accepting any responses until the SSP is approved and locked up in the safe. This is to prevent any bias in favor of a particular offeror. On rare occasions you may get an unexplained two week extension just before the submission date. This can be because of delays in the SSP approval.

The Section M and SSP evaluation factors are the same, however, in that they identify the various *disciplines* against which your response will be scored.

Source Selection Evaluation Board (SSEB): The SSEB is the group of evaluators who actually score your response against the SSP "standards," and is subdivided into the various subpanel disciplines germane to the product or service. Your response will be broken down into packages that are handed to the SSEB subpanel appropriate to that discipline. In this way, technical subpanels evaluate your technical story, management subpanels evaluate your management plan, and a logistics subpanel evaluates your logistics story. If you *have not* followed the solicitation instructions for organizing your response in accordance with the solicitation Section L, the diverse elements of your response cannot be broken down and distributed to the appropriate subpanel, and will not be evaluated. In fact, your response will be rejected at the initial assessment by the Contracting Officer upon opening your package.

Source Selection Advisory Council (SSAC): The SSAC is an independent group of high level officials that advises the SSA on special issues like funding, political aspects, Executive Branch of the Government, and international implications. These may or may not significantly influence the SSA's contract award decision.

Source Selection Authority (SSA): For every contract award, there is a single individual who makes the final decision and contract award. The larger the dollar amount and the higher the political implications, the higher will be the "pay grade" of the SSA. Small contracts may be decided at a relative low level at the contracting command, but large programs may be decided as high as the Secretary of Defense.

Government Ombudsman and Protests: For every solicitation the government identifies an impartial agent to whom dissatisfied bidders may take their grievances in accordance with specifically defined rules for protest. Needless to say, this is not the wish of the contracting office, but is mandated by federal law. The contracting officer wants to avoid any grounds for protests because it is an expensive, time consuming, operation. But the legal provisions are there if you believe that you have been treated unfairly. Be aware, however, that the government will not be favorably disposed to your case, and it could make the difference in a tightly competed competition.

Section M Evaluation Factors for Award

The solicitation evaluation factors may be broken down into various Factors and Subfactors germane to the specific product or service being solicited. The following is an example of some of the **Specific Evaluation Factors** and **Subfactors** for an aircraft solicitation:

- Technical *(factor)*
  o Airframe *(subfactor)*
  o Propulsion System *(subfactor)*
  o Flight Control System *(subfactor)*
  o Weapons Systems *(subfactor)*
- Management *(factor)*
  o Program Management *(subfactor)*
  o Systems Engineering *(subfactor)*
  o Subcontract Management *(subfactor)*
  o Quality assurance *(subfactor)*
- Integrated Logistics Support (ILS) *(factor)*
  o Training *(subfactor)*
  o Logistics Support
- Cost (factor)
  o Unit/Life Cycle Cost *(subfactor)*

The Specific Evaluation Factors really identify only the various disciplines that will likely make up the Government's SSEB, and are a clue as to the makeup of your formal review teams. Their relative weighting will indicate roughly how many pages you should devote to each topic.

In addition to these specific evaluation factors, this section will also include a number of **General Evaluation Factors** and **Subfactors** that are applied throughout the solicitation evaluation:

- The General Evaluation Factors
  o Past Performance
  o Offeror's Financial Stability
  o Risk Assessment and Mitigation Plan

The actual evaluations of all these factors is conducted through the application of **Assessment Criteria**:

- Assessment Criteria
  o Understanding the Requirements
  o Soundness of Approach
  o Compliance With Requirements
  o Specific Areas of Interest

The Assessment Criteria defines the specific aspect of your response in each Specific Evaluation Factor that the evaluators will use for scoring. For each "standard" of the SSP, the evaluators will score your understanding of the requirements, the soundness of your approach, and your compliance with the requirements. The RFP may also identify areas of interest specific to the detail requirements of the product or service.

Evaluation Factors Definitions

You must understand that these assessment criteria will be applied so you *must* provide this information in every section of your response, or that section may be scored "Non-responsive, non acceptable."

Understanding the Requirements: The response shall present evidence of the offeror's appreciation of the basic requirements and their interrelationships. It shall demonstrate his familiarity with the detailed aspects of the problems involved and shall clearly show his understanding of the Specifications and the Statement of Work.

Compliance with Requirements: The response shall present evidence that the offeror's proposed design complies with all stated technical, cost, and schedule requirements.

Soundness of Approach: The response shall demonstrate a reasonable approach, providing confidence that the end result will probably be attained. It should indicate past research exploring possible approaches, and explain why the proposed approach is better for the Government than any other. Any uncertainties should be identified, and a plan described, or at least outlined, as to how the offeror plans to resolve those issues.

Additional Definitions

You must provide enough factual data to convince the evaluators of the soundness of your approach. In addition, you must identify all of the risks that the Government thinks exist, and how you will mitigate them to bring the program to fruition on time, within the budget, and meeting all requirements.

Quality of Substantiating Data: The offeror must provide comprehensive, accurate data to substantiate his schedule and performance claims. These data will be analyzed to determine the validity of the offeror's claims.

Risk Assessments: The offeror must identify all cost, schedule, and performance risks, and categorize them as "low," "moderate," or "high," in accordance with standard DoD definitions. The Offeror must also describe the planned "special contractor emphasis" and provisions for "close Government monitoring" required to overcome the risks.

SSEB Sample Organization

Each SSEB team will be divided into panels germane to the specific evaluation factors. These teams will be subdivided into panels and sub-panels qualified to understand and assess the lower level elements, factors, sub-factors, items, sub-items, etc. For the aircraft example shown above, the SSEB could include, but not be limited to, the following makeup:

- Technical Panel
  o Airframe Subpanel
  o Propulsion System Subpanel

- o Flight Control System Subpanel
- o Weapons Systems Subpanel
- o Performance Subpanel
- o Environmental Subpanel
- o Payload/Range Subpanel
- Management Panel
  - o Program Management Subpanel
  - o Systems Engineering Subpanel
  - o Subcontract Management Subpanel
  - o Quality assurance Subpanel
  - o System Safety Subpanel
- Logistics Panel
  - o Training Subpanel
  - o Logistics Support Subpanel
- Cost Panel
  - o Unit/Life Cycle Cost Subpanel
  - o Cost Reasonableness Subpanel
  - o Should Cost Subpanel
- Other Panels
  - o Safety Subpanel
  - o MANPRINT Subpanel (for US Army submissions)
  - o Risk Mitigation Plan Subpanel

The Cost Panel evaluation differs significantly from the other panels: your cost volume is "evaluated" but not "scored." It assesses whether the costs/pricing is reasonable for the work being performed, and, based upon your DCAA-audited costs, and what it will probably cost to complete your Contract Statement of Work (CSOW). Here's the rub: Your price will be evaluated upon this "should cost" value, not upon the price you quote in your response! If you quote $10 M in your response, and the Government Cost Panel computes that it will probably cost $12 M to do everything promised in your CSOW, then you will be evaluated at $12 M. Therefore, if you suspect that the Government "should cost" values will differ from your quote, then you must explain why. The trap some contractors fall into is when the response CSOW has been written and priced, and top-management at the last minute decrees that "…$12 M is too much, reduce the price to $10 M." But then there is a disconnect between the CSOW and the pricing, that will bite you in the end. Pricing and CSOW must be consistent.

The Evaluation Standards Against Which Your Response Is Evaluated and Scored

The government Source Selection Plan (SSP) defines the specific criteria for which your response shall be assessed. There will be **Quantitative Standards** for areas that can be given specific, quantitative numbers, and **Qualitative Standards** for areas that cannot be numerically defined. The standards format for these assessment criteria are defined in the SSP in the following formats:

Example Quantitative Standard

AREA: Operational Utility
ITEM: Mission Performance Characteristics
FACTOR: Payload/Range
DESCRIPTION: This factor is defined as the payload which can be carried, considering the basic design gross weight, in a given range, when operational utilization of the aircraft is considered. (Load Factor 2.5)
STANDARD: The standard is met when the response shows that at a weight not exceeding the basic design gross weight, the aircraft is capable of transporting a payload of:
  a. 30,000 lbs. for a 2800 nm distance
  b. 48,000 lbs. for a 1400 nm distance

Example Qualitative Standard

AREA: Management
ITEM: System Integration
FACTOR: System Safety
DESCRIPTION: The proposed system safety program will be evaluated for adequacy in effecting the design of changes or modifications to the baseline system to achieve special safety objectives. The evaluation will consider the specific tasks, procedures, criteria, and techniques the contractor proposes to use in the system safety program.
STANDARD: The standard is met when the response:
  a. Defines the scope of the system safety effort and supports the stated safety objectives.
  b. Defines the qualitative analysis techniques proposed for identifying hazards to the depth required.
  c. Describes procedures by which engineering drawings, specifications, test plans, procedures, test data, and results will be reviewed at appropriate intervals to ensure safety requirements are specified and followed.

This qualitative example SSP instruction illustrates an evaluation standard that is not specifically quantified. Each of these criteria will also be scored as to the offeror's Understanding of the Requirements, Soundness of Approach, and Compliance with the Requirements. Risk will also be assessed across the board.

You can build in credibility for qualitative standards by describing the published company policies or procedures you will utilize for these factors. Remember that to be acknowledged as a "process," it must be documented, repeatable, and institutionalized throughout your company and flowed down to your teammates, subcontractors, and suppliers. Certifications, such as ISO certification for Quality Assurance, is a huge plus.

Note that the Areas, Items, Factors, Subfactors, and Descriptions in the SSP normally track the solicitation Section M Evaluation Factors for Award very closely. Only the Standards are divulged.

Also note that in a well prepared solicitation, there is direct correlation between the Section L Instructions to Offerors and Section M. This is so that if the offeror organized its response in 100% compliance with the Section L, it will also be organized in direct compliance with Section M and the SSP evaluation and scoring process.

Risk Assessment

Before responses are evaluated, your customer's Program Manager is briefed on all of the program risks. This list will probably be longer than your list. The evaluators will check whether you have identified those risks and have defined a plan to mitigate them. If your risk assessment differs from theirs, then "…you don't understand the problem," which is a major specific evaluation criterion.

A major failure with many responses occurs when they don't identify the risks that the Government thinks exist because they don't want to "frighten the customer." Don't underestimate your customer's intelligence. If the evaluators don't know the risks of your program, you can bet that your competitors will point them out (as you should point out the risks of their offerings).

Some risks are inherent to the program and apply to all bidders. If so, then discuss these as "Ghost Stories" to alert the evaluators to watch out for how your competitors address them. Some risks apply only to you and your offer. Be candid and explain how you will mitigate them. If you think your risks are different from the Government's then explain why, Don't ignore perceived risks because you "don't want to scare the customer."

Inherent Risk: An inherent risk is one caused by program requirements or constraints, state-of-the-art limitations, or physical laws. Inherent risks affect all Offerors and must be mitigated by all offerors. If you identify an inherent risk, the Government agrees that it is an inherent risk, and the other offerors do not address them, they may be scored "RED" because they "do not understand the problem."

Contractor Risk: These risks are caused by a specific offeror's real or Government-perceived deficiency(ies). This can be *your own risk*—that you *must* prove you will mitigate, or a *competitor's risk* that you bring to the evaluators' attention through a "ghost story" in your response.

Risk Assessment Matrix

The DoD risk level is determined from a combination of its likelihood to occur, and its impact to the program (cost, schedule, or performance) should it occur. The government uses the following matrix for determining the risk level, so you should use it also.

Occurr-ence	Negligible No effect on program	Minor Small cost/ sched. increase	Moderate Moderate, some reqts. not met	Serious Major, min. reqts. Not met	Critical Program failure
1-10% Very unlikely	Low risk	Low risk	Low risk	Moderate Risk	Moderate Risk
11-40% Unlikely	Low risk	Low risk	Moderate Risk	Moderate Risk	High Risk
41-60% Half the time	Low risk	Moderate Risk	Moderate Risk	Moderate Risk	High Risk
61-90% Likely	Moderate Risk	Moderate Risk	Moderate Risk	High Risk	High Risk
91-100% Very likely	Moderate Risk	High Risk	High Risk	High Risk	High Risk

Risk Definitions

High Risk: Likely to cause significant serious disruptions of schedule, increase in cost, or degradation of performance, even with special   contractor emphasis and close Government monitoring.

Moderate Risk: Can potentially cause some disruption of schedule, increase in cost, or degradation of performance. However, special contractor emphasis and close Government monitoring will probably be   able to overcome difficulties.

Low Risk: Has little potential to cause disruption of schedule, increase in cost, or degradation of performance Normal contractor effort and normal Government monitoring will probably be able to overcome difficulties.

No Risk: No program impact. Monitored as part of the normal project management process.

Note that if you claim **low risk**, you are telling your customer that you will conduct "business as usual." If you indicate that any risk is **"moderate"** or **"high,"** then you must clearly identify the "special contractor emphasis" and provisions for "close Government monitoring" that you will provide, including your risk mitigation plan, the metrics you will monitor to control its mitigation, and your closure criteria and schedule.

Note, also, that all risks are related to cost, schedule, and performance. Every word in your responses must relate to cost, schedule, or performance.

US Army MANPRINT Requirements

When responding to US Army solicitations, in addition to everything else, you must also address MANPRINT. This is an acronym for MANpower and PeRsonnel INTegration, and its purpose is to ensure that the system is **designed for the warfighter**, and not to require the **warfighter to man the system**.

This requirement corrects a potentially fatal flaw in the materiel acquisition process, which is the lack of attention paid to soldier performance early in system design and development. Technology employed in a vacuum is not the solution. Soldiers can be overburdened by high-technology weapon systems and force effectiveness can suffer as a result. When the high technology weapons systems of today's modern army are designed and developed by brilliant scientists and engineers, the common soldier, frequently with only a grade school education, cannot utilize them effectively and efficiently to their full potential—in some case, they can't use them at all!

The US Army will no longer accept highly sophisticated systems, developed by highly educated scientists and engineers, that are too complex for its soldiers to operate effectively in the heat of battle. It's not the right tool if the warfighter can't use it.

Seven Tenets of MANPRINT

There are seven aspects of MANPRINT that you must address in your responses to US Army solicitations because the SSEB will apply these criteria throughout all sections of your response.

1. **Manpower:** The number of human resources, both men and women, military and civilian, required and available to operate and maintain Army systems.
2. **Personnel:** The aptitudes, experiences, and other human characteristics necessary to achieve optimal system performance.
3. **Training:** The requisite knowledge, skills, and abilities needed by the available personnel to operate and maintain systems under operational conditions.
4. **Human Factors Engineering:** The comprehensive integration of human characteristics into system definition, design, development, and evaluation to optimize the performance of human-machine combinations.
5. **System Safety:** The inherent ability of the system to be used, operated, and maintained without accidental injury to personnel.
6. **Health Hazards:** Inherent conditions in the operation or use of a system (e.g., shock, recoil, vibration, toxic fumes, radiation, noise) that can cause death, injury, illness, disability, or reduce job performance of personnel.
7. **Soldier Survivability:** The characteristics of a system that can reduce fratricide, detectability and probability of being attacked, as well as minimize system damage, soldier injury, and cognitive and physical fatigue.

Scoring Method

The SSEB will use the following definitions in its evaluation:

a. Deficiency: A material failure of a response to meet a Government requirement or a combination of significant weaknesses in a response that increases the risk of unsuccessful contract performance to an unacceptable level.

b. Significant Weakness: A flaw that appreciably increases the risk of unsuccessful contract performance.

c. Weakness: A flaw in the response that increases the risk of unsuccessful contract performance.

d. Strength: An aspect of an Offerors response that has merit or exceeds specified performance or capability requirements in a way that will be advantageous to the Government during contract performance.

e. Significant Strength: An aspect of an Offeror's response that has appreciable merit or appreciably exceeds specified performance or capability requirements in a way that will be appreciably advantageous to the Government during contract performance.

f. Uncertainty: Any aspect of a non-cost/price factor response for which the intent of the Offeror is unclear (e.g., more than one way to interpret the offer or inconsistencies in the response indicating that there may have been an error, omission or mistake).

g. Adverse Past Performance: Past Performance information that supports a less than satisfactory rating from sources where the information is from other than formal rating systems.

The SSEB will use a rating and color coding scheme such as the following:

COLOR	RATING	DESCRIPTION
BLUE	OUTSTANDING	Response meets requirements and indicates an exceptional approach and understanding of the requirements. Strengths far outweigh any weaknesses. Risk of unsuccessful performance is very low.
PURPLE	GOOD	Response meets requirements and indicates a thorough approach and understanding of the requirements. Response contains strengths which outweigh any weaknesses. Risk of unsuccessful performance is low.
GREEN	ACCEPTABLE	Response meets requirements and indicates an adequate approach and understanding of the requirements. Strengths and weaknesses are offsetting or will have little or no impact on contract performance. Risk of unsuccessful performance is no worse than moderate.

YELLOW	MARGINAL	Response does not clearly meet requirements and has not demonstrated an adequate approach and understanding of the requirements. The response has one or more weaknesses which are not offset by strengths. Risk of unsuccessful performance is high.
RED	UNACCEPTABLE	Proposal does not meet requirements and contains one or more deficiencies. Proposal is un-awardable.

A score will be assigned to the SSP Standard for each factor, and a color-coded chart will be submitted to the SSA for his/her decision. Note that, although the SSA does not see the responders' names, he/she will have a pretty good guess from reading the Executive Summary (which all SSAs do).

Standard	Understand. Reqmts.	Sound. of Approach	Compliance with Reqmts.	Risk
Std. A	Green	Green	Red	Yellow
Std. B	Blue	Green	Green	Blue
Std. C	Yellow	Yellow	Purple	Green
Std. D	Green	Yellow	Green	Yellow

The SSEB is the only Government group that actually scores your response against the SSP standards. It may use a numerical scoring system (1 though 5; 1 through 10; 1 through 100, etc.) or a symbol scoring system (+, 0, -), or this color code. Whether the initial scoring is done symbolically or numerically, these low level scores are converted to color codes as they are summed/averaged up to the next higher levels.

Individual Subfactors are averaged to color code their parent Factors, and Factors are averaged together to code their parent Areas. So three green and two yellow Subfactors will result in a green Factor.

EXCEPT: four greens and only one red will become *red*! One red score in any Subfactor or Factor will degrade the entire Factor or Area.

In the above example, Standard A would receive a red score; Standard B would receive either a green or blue score, depending upon the whim of the evaluators, Standard C would receive a yellow, and Standard D would receive either a yellow or green.

The Contracting Officer will determine what level of scoring determines the Competitive Range. This is important, because any response determined to be in the Competitive Range must be given a chance to respond to Deficiency Reports or Requests for Clarification. The Competitive Range depends upon several factors, including who is responding, and how many responses are received. If (say) 20 responses are received the Competitive Range will be set fairly high to narrow the field. If only (say) three responses are received, all three will probably be judged "in the competitive range" or there will be no price competition.

How Evaluators Read and Evaluate Responses

Response authors and managers frequently complain that the structure specified in the RFP Section L, Instructions to Offerors, interferes with the way they want to tell their story. The story doesn't "flow." Not to worry: the "story" doesn't have to flow, because the evaluators don't "read the story," they look for specific answers to the questions listed in their SSP. This is not to say that your writing can be disjointed, poorly written, or grammatically incorrect—it must have some logical sequencing but not necessarily specific "flow" within the constrained page budget. The main objective is to answer the questions as defined in Section L, IAW the format and organization specified in Section L, address the factors listed and/or implied in Section M, and explain "how" you will satisfy the contractual tasks specified in the Statement of Work or Statement of Objectives.

Evaluators look for short cuts, particularly when evaluating many or large responses. When they first get the responses they usually skim them all in order to understand "the norm." Then they reread them for content and scoring. Therefore the response must be "skimmable" and create a  positive impression from elements that stand out during their skimming. They read the Cover Letter, Executive Summary, Section Introductions, Graphics, Graphic Captions, and bullet lists. Some may jump from Graphic to Graphic and read Graphic Captions (Comic Book Reader). Body text is the last item read, if read at all.

Evaluators are forbidden by the FARs to evaluate one response against another—they must evaluate and score each response solely in accordance with the Source Selection Plan standards, independently of all the other responses. Once they have an idea of the overall responses they re-read for scoring.

Two to four times the people you know will read and evaluate your response—all give points, and their evaluations start from the bottom up. Your response must convince the evaluators at the bottom and sustain itself as it goes up the organization.

The FARs' objective is to make the evaluations and scoring objective, but, let's face it, the evaluators are only human, and subjectivity can easily creep in. It will be harder to convince an evaluator that you are good if he or she already thinks you are not.

Three Kinds of Response Evaluators

Experts: 'These evaluators know and understand the technical issues, and expect to see the technical jargon. They get bored with too much obvious explanation. They know that they know.

Laymen: These evaluators do not know the technical issues and rely upon experts for technical details. They know that they do not know, and usually do not cause problems.

Alleged Experts: These evaluators have heard the technical jargon and think they know and understand the details. They know not that they know not. If they do not understand something, they blame the writers. These evaluators cause the problems.

Responses must communicate accurately to the laymen, not talk down to the experts, and keep the alleged expert on the right track. All three are important and must be addressed. Use the technical jargon for the experts, and expect the laymen to ask for explanations from the experts. For the alleged experts, use the technical terms in a self-explanatory context to "gently" educate them. Then they feel good because they now understand the technical issues.

> *War Story:*
> *For one response, when I conducted the pre-RFP Competition Data Base (CDB) assessment, we analyzed the Government's organization. My client reported that its customer's technical and management personnel were unsophisticated, but its logistics personnel were fully qualified and on top of the issues. We decided, therefore, to write the logistics volume to the "experts," and the technical and management volumes to the "alleged experts." These were powerful insights before the RFP was released.*

Government evaluators are human. Suppose there are six submissions, and the evaluators spend (say) three days on each one. That's 18 days away front their real jobs! They don't want to be there, any more that you wanted to be away from your real job writing the submission. Making it easier for them to find the answers they are looking for will improve your win probability.

PART II – ANALYZING GOVERNMENT SOLICITATIONS

*How to analyze Government solicitations to be
100% compliant with format requirements and
100% responsive to program requirements*

Analyzing the Solicitation – RFP

US Department of Defense solicitations are normally released in the following format:

Cover Letter: The first thing you might see in a solicitation is a Cover Letter. This explains some aspects of the solicitation and what the government wants to accomplish. It may or may not give you useful information for planning your program and writing your response

Information to Offerors or Quoters, DD Form 1707: If a DD Form 1707 is provided, you must sign this and return it immediately to let the Government know whether you intend to respond. This will let them know about how many responses to expect and to plan for.

Standard Form 33 -- Solicitation, Offer and Award: The DD Form 33   names the solicitation (sort of), tells you the issuing agency, solicitation number, RFP release date, response submission instructions, and classification. It also provides a table of contents of the solicitation. The RFP number comprises a number that identifies the issuing agency, the year, "R" for "RFP," and a sequence number from that agency. It identifies the Contracting Office and his/her contact information, who is the *sole and only contact* you may have with that government agency during the response period. The solicitation number (for RFPs, RFIs, and RFQs) will be a number such as: **W15QKN-15-R-0019**. The first part **(W15QKN)** identifies the solicitation issuing office, the second part **(-15-)** identifies the year (i.e. 2015), the third part **(-R-)** identifies this as an RFP, and will be changed to **-C-** upon contract award, and the last part **(-0019)** identifies the sequence number of the solicitations offered by that agency during that year.

Amendment of Solicitation/Modification of Contract, SF 30: If changes or additions are made by the government after the solicitation is released, it will do so through amendments. The amendment will usually be summarized in an SF 30, and changed solicitation pages are usually attached. After solicitations are formally released, official modifications can only be made by formal amendments, not other communications, such as questions and answers. Sometimes the government will attach a complete copy of the modified solicitation, and you must figure out what has changed. Fortunately, most government agencies are more considerate and just attach the change pages with revision bars in the margins.

Part I - The Schedule: This part presents Sections A, B, C, D, E, F, G, and H.

Section A – Solicitation/Contract Form is a continuation of the SF 33. It may include an Executive Summary of what the government expects. You should consider addressing the most important of these in your Executive Summary.

Section B -- Supplies or Services and Prices/Costs provides the pricing forms for each line item to be purchased and the year it is to be provided. It lists the Contract Line Items (CLINs) and Subcontract Line Items (SLINs) identifying the items, quantities, and deliveries that you must price. Sometimes it includes the delivery destinations.

Section C - Description/Specs./Work Statement specifies the actual work that you must complete on the contract. Sometimes this is only a general overall statement of the work expected, and the detailed work is specified in an attachment instead, as a Statement of Work (SOW) or Statement of Objectives (SOO). If it is a SOO then you must define the work that you believe with deliver those objectives.

Section D - Packaging and Marking specifies how you must package and mark each delivery.

Section E - Inspection and Acceptance identifies how and where the government will inspect and accept your deliveries.

Section F - Deliveries or Performance specifies what you will deliver, where it must be delivered, and when it must be delivered. This is a good place to find the information to prepare your contract schedule.

Section G - Contract Administration Data identifies the contracting office and requires you to fill out the information on your company. It may also identify the type of contract planned (i.e., CPFF, CPIF, FFP, etc). There are places where an authorized representative of your company, usually the president, signs to make the contract legally binding.

Section H - Special Contract Requirements specifies any unique actions you must complete germane to this specific solicitation after contract award. If not specifically required by Section L, then it's *not necessary* to address these, but is would be wise to mention them in a statement such as: "During contract work, we will comply with all Special Contract Clauses specified in RFP Section H" and you might address specifically any that seem especially important to your customer, such as warranty requirements.

Part II - Contract Clauses: This part presents Section I, which is an exhaustive list of Government "boilerplate" specifications that you need not address directly in your response. These are mostly specifications describing things you must do after contract award. Some of these requirements are the result of various lobby groups in order to benefit their constituents. Some of these might affect your actions and costs. Uncomfortable, perhaps, but you will be stuck with these after contract award.

Part III – List Of Documents, Exhibits, And Other Attachments: This part presents Section J.

Section J - List of Attachments is a table of contents listing of all the solicitation documents. You need to review this section to ensure that you have all of the necessary solicitation documents, including attachments, in order to be 100% responsive to the solicitation.

Part IV – Representations and Instructions: This part presents Sections K, L, and M.

Section K - Representations, Certifications, and Other Statements of Offerors: You do not address this in your response directly, but you must complete the certifications in the spaces indicated for your response, and include it with your Model Contract. There will be places where you need to fill in the blanks with specific information.

Section L - Instructions. Conditions, and Notices to Offerors: This section provides instructions about organizing and submitting your response. Perhaps the most important sections in the entire solicitation are the sections specifying the response format, page limitations, and specific instructions for what is to be presented in each response section. The importance of these two subsections cannot be over emphasized: The first thing that the government Contracting Officer does after he/she opens your response, is to verify that you have followed the organization specified. If your response does not follow these instructions *exactly*, then the Contracting Office *tosses* your response or *returns it to you unread!* The evaluators never see it! This is because the Government's Source Selection Plan that will be used to score your response is set up in accordance with this response organization. If your response does not conform to this organization, the evaluators cannot apply their SSP scoring sheets. The second thing he/she does is count the pages in each section. Any pages exceeding the specified page limitations are deleted and the evaluators never see them. Do not try to circumvent the page limitations with clever page numbering—they don't look at these, they count the pages. Note that some sections, such as tables of contents, list of illustrations, divider pages, and cross references are not included in the page limitations. Sometimes other sections, such as past performance, resumes, cost volume, and Integrated Master Schedule are excluded from the page limitations. You should page number these sections with a discriminating scheme, such as Roman numerals, with the added notation: "Not included in page count."

Section M - Evaluation Factors for Award: This section explains how the government will evaluate and score your response—sort of. Actually, it only tells you the makeup of the Source Selection Evaluation Board, and the disciplines by which you will be evaluated. This is important, because if you include information in a response section that is not germane to that Section M discipline, the evaluators who should see that information will not see it. Frequently this section will hint at the relative importance of the various sections. This information can serve as a general guide in allocating page budgets to the various response sections. It will usually state something to the effect that "...technical and management are more important than cost..." don't you believe it: Price is *always* number one! And don't be fooled by a statement that: "Life Cycle Cost is more important than initial cost." No current government administration will spend more of its money so that a future administration can save money!

Attachments: The attachments provide the real "meat" of what the Government wants, and can be almost anything. The list here is a good indication of what you may find including the WBS, SOW, SOO, PWS, Data Items (CDRLs), System Specifications, DD -254, DD-253, and Classification Guide.

The **Work Breakdown Structure (WBS)** identifies the pricing categories by which the government will accrue cost information. Sometimes a detailed WBS is provided, and sometimes just a high level WBS. Remember that your "system" may be a "subsystem" to a larger solicitation and you must develop a Contract Work Breakdown Structure (CWBS). Note that your WBS Level 1 may be the parent system's WBS Level 2 or 3. MIL-HDBK-881 provides excellent guidelines for constructing a WBS.

Statement of Work (SOW): The SOW defines exactly the work that you much complete in order to meet the contract requirements and be paid. Sometimes the SOW is provided in the solicitation Section C, and sometimes it's provided as an attachment. Either way, follow it exactly. You may add to this as needed to discriminate your offering, but do not ignore any of it. Address each task and explain how you will do it better than your competitors. The SOW may encompass technical, management, logistic, and data tasks.

Statement of Objectives (SOO): Sometimes the Government just tells you what it wants the product or service to do in a SOO, and you must define the actual Contract Statement of Work (CSOW) to meet those requirements. This is an excellent place to discriminate against your competitors.

Performance Work Statement (PWS): Sometimes there is a PWS, in which the Government identifies the performance criteria that it will use to assess your contracted work. Your performance on each CSOW task will be evaluated in order to qualify for payment for each task.

Data Item Description (DID). The government runs on paper reports, and is obsessed with documenting everything you do. The solicitation specifies this documentation in its Data Item Descriptions (DIDs), specifically in its Contract Data Requirements List (CDRLs). The CDRLs identify the reports that are required, the submission schedules and distribution, and any tailoring to the referenced DID for this specific solicitation.

System or Performance Specifications: If the product is to perform some sort of operation, detailed specifications will be provided. Usually these requirements are addressed in your Technical Volume, and space can be saved by the use of tables, charts, and figures.

Security Classification, DD Form 254: If any part of the work will be classified, a DD Form 254 will identify the classification and provide a classification guide with instructions of what is to be classified and to what level. This guide itself will be unclassified.

DD-253 and Classification Guide. If the solicitation is Department of Defense (DOD) classified, (i.e., secret, top secret, special access, NOFORN, or black) then the instructions for complying with the DOD handling requirements are defined here.

Bear in mind that solicitations, like responses, are prepared by committees, each with its own interests. The technical people are focused upon performance, the management people are focused upon how the program will be managed, the logistics people are focused upon supply and support, and the bean counters are focused upon cost, schedule, and performance reporting. Because of this, there are bound to be overlaps among the various sections of the solicitation. You will discover duplications, conflicts, and additional requirements scattered throughout the solicitation.

In the following example from an actual RFP, responding only to the Section L—and even with the SOW—would miss additional critical information provided in the RFP Section H, Special Contract Provisions, and other Data Items. This could result in failure to respond to several requirements and to underestimating travel expenses by as much as $100,000. This emphasizes the need to read the entire RFP, cover to cover, in order to "comply with all requirements."

Section L	SOW - Reviews	Section H	CDRLs
Program reviews up to 3 days each Identifies USAF, Navy, and Army bases for informal reviews	Program Reviews 5 at Contractor's site Government gives 3 weeks' notice Reviews every 4 months Contractor agenda 2 weeks before review 1 set viewgraphs plus 75 hard copies Contractor Summary within 30 days Additional informal reviews as needed	4 Reviews at Government facilities (Additional information on subjects) May be 6 conferences, and an Annual Symposium in Washington, D.C. with 4 Contractor attendees	May use electronic mail View-graphs in 1 week, hard copy at review Conference minutes in 2 weeks, electronic mail OK

Analyzing the Solicitation – BAA

Some agencies use other formats for their solicitations. For instance, the Defense Advanced Research Projects Agency (DARPA), uses the Broad Area Announcement (BAA), which is in the following format:

Part One: Overview Information identifies the Federal Agency, solicitation title, contracting information, dates, agency contacts, and whether a classified annex is available.

Part Two: Full Text of Announcement defines what the agency wants.

1.0 Funding Opportunity Description describes the program and what the agency hopes to achieve.

2.0 Award Information identifies whether multiple awards will be made and the period of performance.

3.0 Eligibility Information lists any constraints, qualifications, or actions required of the bidders.

4.0 Application and Submission Information provides general response information and specifics related to response organization and format—similar to DoD RFP Section L, Instructions to Offerors.

5.0 Application Review Information describes how responses will be evaluated—similar to DoD RFP Section M, Evaluation Factors for Award.

6.0 Award Administration Information describes how the agency will notify bidders, provides detailed information on handling classified information, and other information on contracting requirements and information handling.

7.0 Agency Contacts identifies the Government offices responsible for this solicitation.

8.0 Program Information and Operational Characteristics describes the agency management approach and operational requirements—similar to DoD RFP Specifications attachments.

Analyzing Other Solicitation Formats

Basically, all solicitation formats from other federal, state, and local agencies, and foreign governments, comprise the same information—they all define what is wanted, how the response must be prepared and submitted, hints on how the responses will be evaluated, and how the agency will manage the program. Once you understand the basics of how to respond you should have no trouble with any solicitation, even commercial ones.

One basic rule, however, will help you with any solicitation, and that is to fully understand why the agency is soliciting the product or service—what is the problem behind the requirement? Unless you fully understand the problem, you can't really provide a convincing response.

For example, if someone asks you to get them a ¼-inch drill, what do they *really want?* They *don't really want* a ¼-inch drill—they *want a ¼-inch hole in something.* Unless you know what they want a hole in, you can't give them the right kind of drill—do they want to drill a hole in wood, metal, glass, or masonry? Only when you fully understand the problem behind the requirement—why they want the thing—can you offer them the correct product or service.

One way to find out what they *really want* is by "working the customer" far in advance of the solicitation.

PART III – WIN STRATEGIES AND WIN THEMES DEVELOPMENT

*How to develop effective win strategies and themes
to communicate your discriminators*

Win Strategy Development – "Black Hat Review"

Many companies fall into the same trap—they fail to properly analyze an opportunity, and end up wasting valuable B&P money on solicitations they have no chance of winning. Only a thorough analysis of each opportunity can provide the answer to whether it is worth pursuing.

Several years ago I analyzed the proposals I supported. On 23 percent of them I advised my clients to no-bid because I believed they had no chance of winning. All 23 percent lost! A complete waste of time and B&P resources that could have been saved for an opportunity that could win.

That said, there are valid reasons for pursuing an opportunity that you have no chance of winning, one of which it to introduce yourself to a new customer. But even then, you want to do a credible job. Don't shoot yourself in the foot by introducing yourself with a bad, non-responsive submission.

A thorough opportunity analysis will comprise four independent analyses, an analysis of the opportunity itself, i.e., what your customer wants; i.e., an analysis of your customer, i.e., who is your customer, what are his/her wants, needs, and biases, and what will it take for you to win; an analysis of your competitor, i.e., who they are, their strengths and weaknesses, and what they are likely to offer; and an analysis of yourself, i.e. who you are, your own strengths and weaknesses, what you can offer and how well it meets your customer's requirements, the impact to your company for bidding and winning, for bidding and losing, and what your role should be (prime, teammate, subcontractor, vendor, other).

And finally, your resulting win strategy will not be a single strategy, but a complex one encompassing technical, pricing, and political, as well as some other aspect of the opportunity.

The following lists the various contents of a thorough opportunity analysis. Note that as you progress through these actions, you will find duplicates (just skip ahead to the next one) and they will suggest additional considerations that you would not have thought of spontaneously.

Opportunity Analysis

- Is this a real program?
- What is the requested concept/system/ product/service?
- Is this really what the customer wants?
- What is the mission or role of the system/ product/service?
- What are the system/product/service requirements?
- How does this fit your business objectives?

- What are your related company studies/products/ services?
- What are program/market requirements?
- What is your follow-on potential for additional business?
- What are real and perceived cost/schedule/technical risks, and how can you mitigate them?

Customer Analysis

- What is the ultimate user profile?
- What is the profile of the immediate customer?
- What are the customer's key factors?
- What are the programmatic issues?
- Does the customer need help selling this program to its funding authority?
- What are the customer's weighting of issues and receptiveness to trade-offs?
- What are any unresolved customer issues?
- Who or what is really running the show?
- List desired "buzz-words" and topics, as well as "buzz-off" words and topics.
- What will it take to win if you are not the lowest bidder?
- What will win the contract?

Competitor Analysis

- What is the competitive political situation?
- What are the competitive issues?
  - Which can be overcome?
  - How can you overcome them?
  - Which cannot be overcome?
  - What is the impact if you cannot overcome them?
- Who are the competitors?
- What are your competitors' competitive images and influences with the customer?
- What are the likely competitors' solutions?
- What are known and probable competitor's strengths and weaknesses?
- What teaming arrangements are potential among your competitors?
- What are competitive attitudes/programs/issues within the customer's organization or funding authority?
- Is any competitor "wired" to win, and what can you do about it?

Self Analysis

- What are the differences between you and your competitors?
- Do your objectives differ from your competitors?
- What is your experience relative to this?
- What are your strengths relative to this?

- How can you exploit your strengths?
- What are the technical/management/schedule/ financial/program risks?
- What are your weaknesses to be overcome, and how and when will you overcome them?
- What is your probability of success?
- What is your most suitable role?
- What will be the cost of competing?
- What are the short-term consequences of "bid and win," "bid and lose," and "no bid?"
- What are the optimistic, pessimistic, and most likely win probabilities, and your basis for these estimates?
- What elements/features/benefits of your offering need special emphasis?
- Are there reasons for bidding other than to win?

Win Strategy Plan for Bid Decision

After you complete your four analyses you are ready to formulate your various win strategies. Note that your response encompasses all of these, whether you planned them or not! So it's best to plan them deliberately in order to realize their benefits in maximizing your win probability.

- Analyses Summary
- Overview
- Opportunity Analysis Summary
- Customer Analysis Summary
- Competitors Analysis Summary
- Self Analysis Summary
- Overall Analysis Summary
  - o Win Strategy Tree
  - o Business Strategy
  - o System/Product/Service Strategy
  - o Political Strategy
  - o Pricing Strategy
  - o Special Considerations

Obviously, these actions should be completed before a decision is made to respond. This will likely include a number of strategies that you might not have thought were important. For example, your Political Strategy might consider a change of Administration in Washington. This can have a major impact to your program, as was the case in the USAF B-1A program cancellation after Jimmy Carter became President. Once you get the solicitation, you should update your strategies based upon the solicitation Evaluation Factors for Award.

> **War Story:**
> On one response my client had received the RFP and was responding. They had hired another consultant to develop their win strategies. We spent two whole days in a complete waste of time!. The consultant

suggested such actions as co-authoring a technical paper on the subject. I objected, stating that since we already had the RFP, we couldn't talk to the customer, and that we should be strategizing the RFP Section M – Evaluation Factors for Award, but he refused.

Win Strategy Tree

One of the best ways to exploit your win strategies and win themes is by a Win Strategy Tree. It could take the following format:

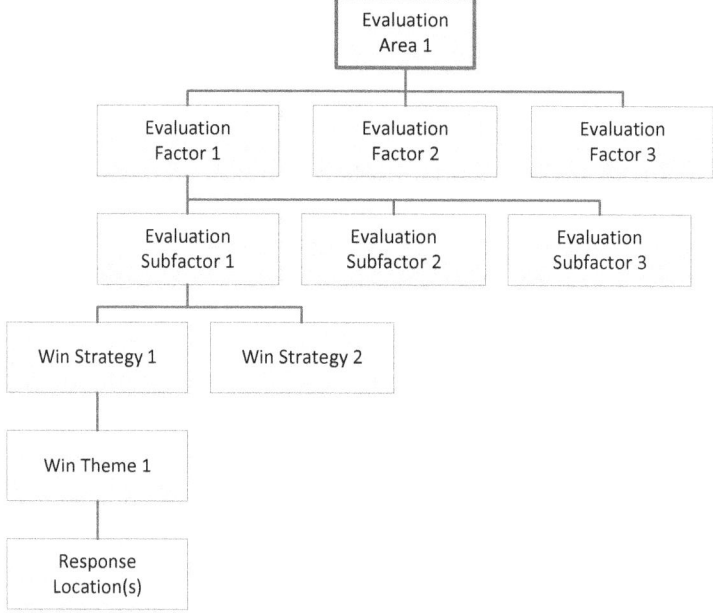

This enables you to define your win themes and present them in your response in the most advantageous location to influence the evaluators.

Features and Benefits—An effective way to influence the evaluators

Your response will include a number of "features" that distinguish you from your competitors and that will "benefit" your customer. Do not leave the benefits up to the evaluators to discover them—point them out in your Features-Benefits presentation.

Features: Specific aspects of your product or service (speed, weight, reliability, in production, delivering this service already, industry leader, etc.)

Benefits: Benefits are specific advantages that your response provides to your customer (low initial or operating cost, improved performance, easy maintenance, low risk, etc.)

Features vs. Benefits: Benefits should address your customer's end objectives for buying If it does not improve cost, schedule, or performance, it's a *feature*, *not a benefit*! For example, the *benefit* of a vacuum cleaner is that it provides a clean house. The *feature* of a vacuum cleaner is that it sucks. If your proposed product or service exceeds any of your customer requirements/specifications, be sure to identify and discuss the specific benefit(s) to your customer of exceeding the requirement. Just exceeding a requirement does not get you the highest score—only if that excess benefits your customer.

Keep asking "so what?" for each feature and benefit until you get to some basic operational need for the new product.

Features and Benefits — SO WHAT?

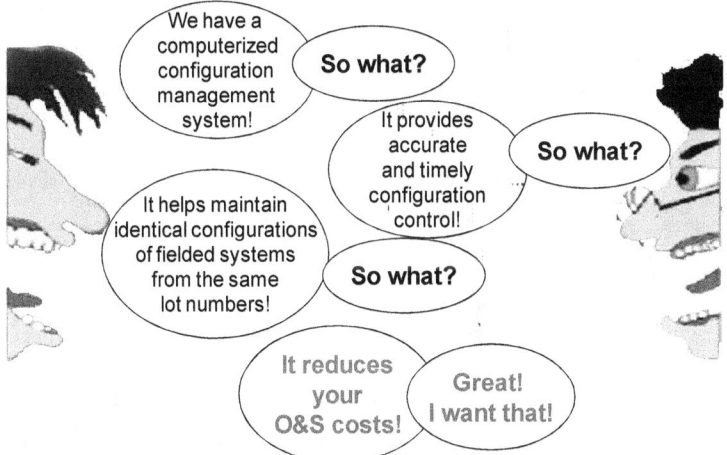

Examples of some features and benefits:

Features	Benefits
Advanced modeling and simulations	Lower development cost; higher reliability
Two identical axial-positive hydraulic drive motors	Simplified maintenance requirements, effective failsafe
History of on time or early deliveries	Dependability; low program risk
Program Manager reporting directly to the General Manager	High program visibility; quicker allocation of resources; more responsive to Customer need

Discriminators

Discriminators are benefits of your offer or solution that:
- Differ from competitors' offers.
- Are important to your customer.

31

- Convince your customer that you can and will deliver on schedule at an acceptable cost.
- All three conditions must be met.

Discriminators are extremely important, but don't ignore things that you do just like your competitors. You must discuss them, as well, so that your competitors do not win a "gotcha" against you.

Think about these criteria relative to how you buy things for your private life. Obviously you don't conduct a formal assessment for everything that you buy, but I'll bet you subconsciously consider these factors, anyway.

- Identify discriminators by understanding your customer, your competitors, and yourself
- Identify both positive and negative discriminators and present them as positively as possible
- Continuously check if a discriminator still discriminates
- Develop discriminators by continuing to define them more specifically, preferably against the main reasons for the solicitation
- Emphasize discriminators that focus on people, experience, performance, and understanding your customer's needs and desires. (These are usually the unique discriminators)

Themes

Win themes or major themes apply at top levels. They usually tie a single, unique discriminator to a critical customer need, such as reduced costs, reduced risks, or the main objective for buying.

Theme Statements link a customer benefit to your discriminators. They tell your customer why they should select you. The most powerful themes contain the most unique discriminators — something they want that no one else offers but you.

An example of a good theme: "Development risk and cost are eliminated by selecting our Widget, the only one in this class that is in current production."

A Winning Discriminator

The following is from (then) Secretary of Defense Dick Cheney's letter to Senator C.S. Bond, dated July 29, 1991, regarding selection of the F/A-18E/F over the F-14. It would be hard for the loser's Congressman to argue against a decision based upon these discriminators.

"In selecting the F/A-18E/F, we considered not only performance and unit price, but also a host of other factors which impact on cost, such as weapon system reliability, maintainability, safety, maintenance costs, squadron manning requirements and cost per flight hour.

"In the final analysis the F/A-18E/F was the clear choice over the F-14. It is three times more reliable, twice as easy to maintain, has a safety record which is fifty percent better, requires about twenty-five percent fewer maintenance personnel, and costs about twenty-five percent less to operate per flight hour. When combined, these factors clearly show that the F/A-18E/F is the more cost-effective aircraft."

The best win themes have three characteristics:

- *unique* to you,
- *important* to your customer,
- *proven* in your response that you can and will deliver at a reasonable cost.

If it is *not*:

- *unique* to you—your customer doesn't have to buy from you,
- *important to your customer*—they won't care,
- *proven in your response*—or they won't believe you.

Then:

- You will lose.

This is the way everyone buys anything. It's the way you buy a shirt, a dress, an automobile, or a house. Government agencies are no different, whether they are buying paper towels, AK-47s, or a new weapons system. In order to win, your offering must be unique to you, important to your customer, and you must prove that you can and will deliver what you promise on time and at a reasonable and acceptable price.

PART IV – ORGANIZING YOUR RESPONSE TEAM AND PLANNING YOUR RESPONSE

How to organize your response team and your response to be most effective and most efficient

Industry Organization and Approach Functions

All companies perform the following response administrative actions, whether by specifically assigned individuals or by only one or two people multi-tasking:

Contracting Officer: Receives solicitation, sole means for all Customer contacts.

Response Administrator: Distributes solicitation to response team and provides the response facility and support.

Capture Manager: Brings opportunities to management attention, determines what it will take to win, and has been (hopefully) "working the customer."

Business Manager: Ensures that resulting contract meets company business objectives.

These are "functions," rather than individual titles. Ideally, in a large organization, each function would be handled by a different individual in order to benefit from the synergism of group discussions, different ideas, and various points of view. In small organizations, many of these functions may be handled by the same person.

All companies also perform the following response actions, whether by specifically assigned individuals or by only one or two people multi-tasking:

Program Manager: Defines the program that will meet Customer requirements.

Response Manager: Ensures that the program is communicated in a winning sales document, meeting all solicitation requirements.

Response Coordinator: Responsible for tracking all response text and graphics, maintains the master response books, and ensures that submission meets all format requirements

These functions are best conducted by different individuals. The benefits of separate people for these functions are that they are all full time jobs, and if they are assigned to a (say) Program Manager, the response sales aspects will suffer and morning meetings will degenerate into technical discussions and "re-inventing" the product or service. Likewise, if the coordinator function is assigned to the Response Manager, he/she will be inundated with the mechanics of getting out the response drafts and the response content will suffer.

These functions will be augmented by a team of writers and illustrators as needed to put the Program Manager's plan into the response as a sales document.

When and How to Ask Questions

Free and open communications are allowed—and encouraged—before a formal solicitation is released, even if there is a draft solicitation. Once the formal solicitation is released by the government Contracting officer, however, all communication doors are closed except through the Contracting Officer identified in the solicitation. And the rules for those communications are strictly defined and strictly enforced. The following describes the communication process once the formal solicitation is released:

Question submission procedures: Questions may be asked on any topic but must be submitted through your Contacting Officer to your customer's Contracting Officer. Each solicitation may define how long questions may be submitted.

Government response procedures: The government Contracting Officer must distribute all questions and answers to all bidders. They will be published anonymously so your company name is not associated with any questions, nor will be the answers.

Answers to questions do not change the solicitation: Note that any published questions and answers (Q&As) are for "information only." Official changes to the solicitation may be made only through a formal Amendment (SF 30).

Government problems in reacting to questions: The government does not want to have to substantially revise solicitations because major changes require complex and time-consuming approvals.

What to ask: The best types of questions are for clarification of program requirements, clarification of response format instructions, and clarification of solicitation contradictions or inconsistencies.

What not to ask: Although you can ask any question you wish, you should use some discretion and common sense. You do not want to "open your Kimono" to your competitors about your response, or show your ignorance to your customer through some stupid, obvious question. You should consider your question's effect upon your customer and your competitors. The obvious questions not to ask are specifics relating to your offering, requesting substantive changes to requirements, or questions that might identify your shortcomings or lack of capability.

Offering suggestions: It is fine to offer suggestions to correct problems that impact your submission and the government evaluation process.

War Story:

On one response I had a major problem in organizing the response. The RFP indicated that the Navy was going to use a semi-automated system to evaluate the responses, so the response paragraph numbers and titles had to exactly match the Section L and Section M numbering. The problem was that the Section L and Section M numbering was inconsistent—there was no way we could comply with the RFP instructions. I drafted a memo to the Navy Contracting Officer, explaining the problem, stating that we wanted to comply but could not because of the inconsistencies. I included a table showing the inconsistent Section L and Section M numbering, and another table with my suggestions to correct the matter. Our contracting office submitted my memo, and we got an almost immediate reply, that said: "You have not only shown us a serious problem, but you have given us the

---

> *solution! This epitomizes the partnership between the Government and Industry.*"

Response Approach Criteria

In order to be <u>accepted</u> for evaluation, your response must:

Be submitted on time: On-time delivery is inviolable—ten seconds late will not be accepted.

Comply with the RFP preparation and submission instructions: Non-compliance with Section L response preparation instructions can disqualify you without evaluators ever seeing your response.

Respond to all RFP response and program requirements: Better to give a bad answer than no answer at all—hope for a clarification request.

To have a chance at <u>winning</u>, your response must also:

- Address the things that are important to the Customer.
- Clearly define your offering.
- Show that you understand the requirements.
- Show the soundness of your approach.
- Show that you comply with all requirements.
- You must show that you know and understand all of the cost, schedule and technical risks, and that you have a more reliable approach to mitigating the risks than your competitors.
- Convince the Customer that if you fail to meet any of his requirements (i.e., non-compliant), your alternate approach to the overall solution is to his benefit.
- Clearly define the things that discriminate you from your competitors (unique to you).
- Convince the Customer of the benefits to his program of your solution (important to the customer).
- Convince the Customer that you can and will deliver as promised at an acceptable cost (credible story).

In order to do all of this there are several competitive things that you must understand and clearly communicate to your response team:

- What does the Customer really want?
- What does the Customer think of you relative to the other offerors?
- What will you have to do to win?
- What will your competitors offer that you can't?
- What will your competitors say about you?
- What should you say about your competitors?
- What are the political factors?

What Will Win

Best Technical & Lowest Price ⟶ **WILL WIN**

2ⁿᵈ Best Technical & Lowest Price ⟶ **CAN WIN**

Best Technical & 2ⁿᵈ Lowest Price ⟶ **CAN WIN**

2ⁿᵈ Best Technical & 2ⁿᵈ Lowest Price ⟶ **WILL LOSE**

Why Your Customer Contact Plan Is Important

"I don't know who you are. I don't know your company. I don't know your company's product. I don't know what your company stands for. I don't know your company's customers. I don't know your company's record. I don't know your company's reputation.

"Now, what was it you wanted to sell me?"

People like to do business with people they know and trust, and government contracting and management people are no different. In spite of the fact that the FARs and the DFARs are enforced in order to make source selection objective, subjectivity creeps in because the source selection people are human. The most ominous words you can ever read in a solicitation are the words: "This will be a Best Value award." For these solicitations, the SSA will select whoever he/she believes to be the best value to the government, regardless of price or other considerations. To counter this, you need to establish a solid rapport with your customer long before the solicitation is even prepared. Because you *are* what your customer *thinks you are!*

When to contact: You should establish a Customer Contact Schedule for contacting all of your potential customers. You can contact them any time until the formal RFP is released, and should be well in advance of any expected solicitations.

Who to contact: You should establish a Customer Contact List of all contract people, program managers, likely users, and other government people with whom you plan to work in the future.

How to contact: Personal contacts are the most effective, and show your customers that they are important to you, and that you are interested in their needs.

What to present: You don't need to divulge details of your proprietary information, but discussing your ideas is great, and explanations of your company's dedication, qualifications, and related programs. If you understand your customer's needs, prepare a "strawman" solicitation and discuss it with him/her.

Where to contact: You can contact your customer at his/her office, at symposia, and at both formal and informal meetings.

Do not assume that your customer knows enough about you to trust you with his/her career decisions. Although the evaluators must evaluate your offering solely on the information in your response, subjectivity can creep in at all levels.

War Story:
I was advising the program manager on an upcoming solicitation. The RFP had not been released, so we could talk with the Air Force program manager. I advised our program manager to draft a statement of work, and meet with the Air Force program manager to discuss our interest and ideas. If the Air Force program manager wouldn't accept a copy of our draft SOW, then he could just "forget" to take it with him when he left. At first he refused, but finally agreed.

He came back from the meeting very excited! He had had a terrific meeting! The Air Force program manager reviewed the draft SOW with him, commenting on each task. Some he was not interested in, others very interested, and some were good ideas that he hadn't thought of. He thanked our guy, and kept a copy of the draft SOW.

Bid & Response (B&P) Budgeting

Solicitation response budgeting is always a difficult compromise between what it will take to prepare and submit a winning response, and what your company bean counters think they can afford. Frequently top management makes this decision, in spite of the fact that top management usually has no idea of the actual, detailed work needed to prepare a winning response.

The Program Manager and the Response Manager should estimate the response budget because only they know the detailed tasks involved. This estimate should be either approved by top-management or the response should be no-bid.

Top-management should not start with a reduced budget because:
- When the program/response runs out of money time will be wasted justifying more money.
- More money will be provided as opposed to stopping.

- A poor, cheaply prepared, losing response would be submitted.

If top-management reduces the budget, when the Program Manager runs out of money, he/she will go back to top-management, who will probably say: "I can't give you the $500,000 you asked for—I'll give you $250,000." When that's gone, the Program Manager will have to spend more time justifying more money, when he/she should really be working on the program. Eventually the money will be provided, a mediocre response will be submitted, or the program will be canceled. Neither of the last two options is likely.

Five Ways to Write a Losing Solicitation

Although there are several ways to prepare a winning solicitation, and many more ways to prepare a losing one, here are five of the losing ways most frequently employed by otherwise well meaning company executives. How many of these have you observed in your company?

1. Underestimate the difficulty and assign the wrong people.
2. Start late.
3. Jump at targets of opportunity.
4. The RFP isn't what the customer really wants–let's tell him in our wonderful response.
5. Don't follow the stupid RFP–it doesn't allow us to tell our story.

What successful companies do and unsuccessful companies do not do—A Case Study

Many years ago, at a Fortune 500 Company, I participated in a thorough study of why our company was losing the large business opportunities. We interviewed our customers, our competitors, and ourselves. Here are the functions that we found most prevalent in the more successful companies:

Structured Management Council: A structured Management Council establishes policies and procedures for identifying winnable opportunities, making bid decisions, and approves program and response management support, review, and approval methods.

Executive Response Assignment: Response assignments are made at the Executive level based upon the most qualified people, not based upon who is not otherwise busy.

Commit Technical and Response Manager up to One Year in Advance: If the opportunity is a large or complex program, key people may be assigned up to a year in advance in order to "work the customer," and develop a responsive and winning solution. This doesn't mean hat they work full time, but that they are dedicated to that opportunity and keep working the customer.

Central Response Organization: Many response organizations are disjointed and spread out at their own desks, even working from home, across the country or in another country with teammates in a "virtual proposal center." This can work—sort of—but the team loses the synergism of co-location. Many times, in a centralized location—meaning within earshot, not down the hall—a discussion will be overheard that affects more than one issue.

Top-Down Price Targets: Frequently, companies ask their engineers and managers to estimate the cost for the work to be done, using Bases of Estimate, and then these costs are summed up the line. These prices will always be high. Top management should not ignore these, but should make an informed estimate of what your competitors should price, what your customer's budget and funding profile will accept, and the minimum price your company is willing to accept from a business standpoint. If the budget is set by top management with no working level intervention, it will always be set too low.

Risk Pricing: Risk pricing has to do with assessing the monetary impact of your price on your company's bottom line, and what unknowns are likely to occur. What delays might run up the costs? What price increases are likely from your suppliers? What price might eliminate you from this competition? Risk pricing is especially important in Firm Fixed Price contracting.

Here are the factors that our study found that contributed to our win ratio of less than one third the national average:

Conclusions:
- Lack of high level response control and operations.
- No top management participation in win strategy development.
- No customer contacts before RFP preparation.
- Lack of price goal at start of response.
- Late program identification.
- Early program identification not supported.
- Top management and Red Team reviews too late.
- Bid-no-bid decisions take too long.
- Lack of system work before design efforts.
- Lack of customer pre-selling and feedback.

Recommendations:
- Centralize response development and preparation with responsibility, authority , and management support.
- Implement a structured Win Strategy program.
- Implement a disciplined marketing intelligence process.
- Improve costing/pricing process.
- Achieve and maintain competitive capability.

The Result of the Study: The recommended corrective action is pretty obvious: fix the problems. The study also found that every other year, for the past 12 years, the company had conducted a similar study and found the same problems, but the company had done nothing. I factiously recommended "Do nothing, and conduct another study in two years." Years later I found that the company did just that! In the mid-1980s the company declared Chapter 11 bankruptcy and major departments were bought by Lockheed-Martin.

V – MANAGING YOUR RESPONSE

How your team that can produce an efficient and effective result.
It's a waste of resources to do something efficiently
if it's not the right thing to do!

Solicitation responses can be managed effectively and efficiently through five distinct tactical phases that key off your overall strategic actions:

> Phase 0 – Strategic Actions
> Phase I – Tactical Actions
> Phase II – Advanced Response Actions
> Phase III – Response Preparation and Submission
> Phase IV – Post-Response Follow-up Actions

Phase 0 – Strategic Actions

During this phase you should identify long range business opportunities that meet your company business objectives, start "working the customer," and assess any lessons learned from similar past responses. You should conduct a rough competitive assessment to identify the opportunity to your top management and obtain initial funding to follow the developing program. You should identify and assign the basic response organization to start planning your program and response approach.

Your Phase 0 planning should result in the following actions:

- Early go-ahead decision completed
- Customer requirements analysis completed
- Strawman solicitation drafted
- Program/Response plans approved
- Concerns and issues identified
- Strawman Executive Summary written
- Management Review completed

Phase I – Tactical Actions

Continue working the customer as soon as you become aware of a customer need. By working with the contracting agency and the user agencies, you can approximate what may be required. Analyze these ideas to identify those that are likely to become formal RFP requirements as opposed to those that are just "wish list" hopes.

Prepare a Strawman solicitation to document these ideas and form guidelines for initiating your advance program work. Depending upon your relationship with your customer, you can even discuss your Strawman RFP with him/her.

Prepare your long range program and response plans and update your competitive assessment.

You will prepare an Executive Summary after you define your program and write your response, but an Executive Summary written early can be a "wish list" of what you need to win, and can provide guidelines of what your engineers and managers should do in order to "make it so."

Obviously, your company management should be closely involved in these long range plans. Your Phase I planning should result in the following actions:

- Draft/Strawman solicitation addressed
- Product Concept Description defined
- Strawman Statement of Work (SOW) approved
- Baseline Work Breakdown Structure (WBS) approved
- Program organization and controls implemented
- Program Plans defined

Phase II – Advanced Response Actions

At this stage, you should refine your Strawman RFP and decide how you will address each issue. You may also have received a draft solicitation. This draft may be a complete solicitation, or it might be just draft Sections L, M, and SOW. This is also when you should also be refining your offering. If the draft solicitation doesn't include a draft SOW you should prepare a strawman SOW to focus your attentions on specific response requirements. Update your competitive assessment. It takes at least 60 days to prepare a good, high quality, winning response. If the solicitation allows you only 45 or 30 days, then you must start before the formal solicitation is released. Avail yourself of any draft RFPs available. Ideally, the draft RFP should include Sections L, M, SOW or SOO, and a draft specification, but this doesn't always happen. Improvise, guesstimate, and talk with your customer.

Your Phase II planning should result in the following actions:

- Response schedule made and approved
- Response plan written and approved
- Product/program tentatively frozen
- Department estimates completed
- Storyboard Outlines reviewed and approved
- Task descriptions prepared and approved
- First drafts prepared and reviewed
- Pricing initiated
- Red Team Review Team organized and committed
- Phase II planning reviewed and approved by top management
- Phase III actions approved

Phase III – Response Preparation and Submission

This Phase III encompasses receipt of your formal solicitation and preparation and submission of your response. Many companies fail to define a realistic response schedule. If it is too short, your authors will ignore it, if it is too long you will not have time to accommodate changes and corrections later in the process. Once you have defined your schedule, your response team must follow it. Some companies mistakenly think it's smart to schedule response completion a week or so in advance of the official submission date. They think this extra "pad" is a clever idea. It's not! It's stupid! Your team recognizes this, and regardless of all your pleading, cajoling, and threatening, your team is not going to meet this fake deadline! Establish a reasonable schedule and enforce it. Your team will respond.

- Response schedule updated and followed.
- Response plan updated and followed.
- Product/program frozen.
- Department estimates finalized and approved.
- Storyboard Outlines reviewed and approved.
- Pink Team Review conducted.
- SOW Task descriptions prepared and approved.
- Various multiple drafts approved.
- Price finalized.
- Red Team Review draft completed and under configuration control of your Coordinator.
- Red Team Review Team conducted.
- Response finalized, approved by top management, printed, quality checked, packaged, and delivered IAW solicitation instructions.

Phase IV – Post-Response Follow-up Actions

Your Phase IV actions, after response submission, can encompass the following actions:

- Response to Customer questions
- Customer debriefing
  - o   Win
  - o   Lose
- Lessons Learned
  - o   Self assessment
    - • Program/response process
  - o   Customer feedback
    - • What you did right
    - • What you did wrong

If you receive questions from your customer, this will give you a chance to greatly improve your win probability.

Always request a debriefing after contract award, even when you win. A customer debriefing after you lose, is obvious, but a customer debriefing after you win is different. Contract winners never protest! This means that you are more likely to get a more candid debriefing after you win, than after you lose. You can find out whether you won *because* of your response or *in spite of it*! Valuable information!

Companies almost always conduct "Lessons Learned" exercises after a response is submitted. This can only identify how your process worked—it can never tell you anything about the quality of your response. A discussion of more productive Lessons Learned assessments is provided in PART XI – POST SUBMISSION ACTIONS.

Response Organizing

Some response team managers think that organizing your proposal is the most difficult part of preparing a response. Nonsense! Organizing your response is the easiest part of the whole process, because the solicitation tells you exactly how.

War Story:

I was briefing the Number 2 executive, the Director of Materiel at Aeronautical Systems Command (ASD) Wright-Patterson AFB. When I said that I always told my clients to follow Section L , Instructions for Proposal Preparation, he actually stood up from the table, and said: "Amen! That's where we tell you what we want to know! If you don't ever even mention *the SOW, we don't care, because you have to complete all the SOW tasks after you sign the contract.*

Obviously you don't want to ignore the SOW, because that's where you distinguish yourself from your competitors. Your response should track the Section L, Section M, and SOW in that order. Your volume, section, and paragraph numbering should track the Sections L and M numbering and titling exactly. This is to ensure that your response is organized to track the evaluators' Source Selection Plan (SSP), and provide "pattern recognition" that makes it easy for the evaluators to find the answers to their questions.

Response Paragraph Numbering

The response file names are the response paragraph numbers and titles (that should track the comparable RFP paragraph numbers and titles), with the author's initials added. The paragraph numbers should include the volume or book number separated by a hyphen. Roman numerals are sometimes used for volume numbers, but computers can sort Roman numerals only up through VIII. So if you have more than eight volumes, it's best to use Arabic numerals for volume numbers. Each time the paragraph is reviewed or revised, the reviewer or author adds his/her initials to the file name. This preserves the original files, and provides information on who has seen the draft, who reviewed it, and what was done in response to the review. For example, for response section/paragraph 1.2 of Volume 1:

    Author originates draft: ....1-1.2 Overview-aod.doc
    Program Manager reviewed: ....1-1.2 Overview-aod-pmr.doc
    Author revises draft: .... 1.2 Overview-aod-pmr-aod.doc
    Program Manager approved:... 1-1.2 Overview-aod-pmr-aod-pmr.doc

These initials will be removed for the Red Team Review draft, and the initials: "RT" will be inserted into the file name to identify it as the official baseline. The initials will be changed for each subsequent draft (i.e., "Pink

Team," "Gold Team," "Final," etc.). Your author and reviewer initials should be added to the file names as described above.

"Stacked changes," i.e., changes made to different file versions at the same time, must be avoided or you will end up with different files that must be consolidated later. Do not review and markup more than one copy at a time.

Illustrations Numbering

All illustrations—photos, tables, flow charts, drawings, etc.—should be numbered in a single Illustrations Numbering scheme in order to simplify referencing and tracking. Authors should get an illustration number from the Response Coordinator. The following is a suggested illustrations numbering scheme:

Initial illustration numbers are simple sequences: 1, 2, 3, etc. They may be assigned a volume prefix: T1, T2, T3,...M1, M2, M3, or the authors' initials. You will discover that illustration numbers will be "out of order" in your response. The first illustration may be number 72, the next one 23, the next one 1, and so one\. Don't worry. The numbers at this point are only to tie the illustration to a paragraph reference. Don't be mislead into using paragraph or section numbers in your illustration numbers. Nothing is more cumbersome that an illustration numbering 1-2.3.4.a! Keep it simple and elegant with 1, 2, 3, 4, and so on. Illustrations may move around to different paragraphs, and paragraph numbers may change. This confuses the illustration tracking if you include paragraph numbers. Your coordinator must maintain a log of where each illustration is placed in your response, and whether the response paragraph number changes. The illustration number will be placed inconspicuously on the illustration and becomes a permanent identifier for future reference. At final book makeup, your coordinator or publications people will use the log to renumber the illustrations to conform with their locations in the response.

Response Document Tracking and Control

Document control should remain with the authors until just before Red Team Review in order to expedite response development, but the Response Coordinator must track progress against the response schedule (i.e., Storyboards, first draft completed, reviewed, revised, approved, etc.). Your Coordinator must keep copies of your developing story in separate directories, say, on the P drive that everyone can access. (i.e., P:\First Draft. P:\Second Draft, etc.). Frequently it will be found that an earlier version of a write-up is better that later versions, and this process enables you to call up the earlier version.

Once the Red Team draft is in work, document control *must be established with your Coordinator* in order to maintain positive control over what is presented to your Red Team Reviewers. If you fail to do this, you will end up with a confusing mixture of old and new material for your Red Team Review. Changes can only be made by your Response Coordinator. Your Coordinator must control your Red Team draft in a separate directory that only he/she can change. Others can review these documents, but cannot make changes!

Your Coordinator must have document control over your final draft for the same reasons.

Response Planning Advice

No one knows better how to plan a response or an attack than military leaders, and there are many similarities between the two:

- You have limited resources that you must use to your best advantage.
- You know some things about your adversary, but not everything you need to know.
- You have an inviolable deadline.
- Losing may be disastrous.

Proposal Secrets of Attila The Hun

Who better than Attila The Hun to plan and wage a successful campaign?

OK, Attila never wrote proposals, but he did manage to persuade hundreds of thousands of Huns to band together, which they didn't want to do, to pursue a common cause and win victories (does this sound like your proposal team?). His armies appeared to the powerful Roman Empire as a rag-tag mob of barbarians (need I say more?), but he managed to overthrow the Romans, the most powerful military might in the world (the incumbent)!

How did he do it? According to Wes Roberts, PhD., in his enlightened book *Victory Secrets of Attila The Hun* (Doubleday, 1993), he followed several common sense maxims, developed by noticing what he observed, not by what he wanted to see. As Yoga Berra said, "You can observe a lot just by watching."

How would he succeed today on proposals? He would be as formidable now as he was then. Here are ten of his maxims, which I have translated into proposalese: See what you think.

Battle Maxims	Proposal Maxims
Wise chieftains never engage their tribes in marginal battles. It costs too much, and the rewards are usually not worth the tribe's time and energy	Don't waste your time, energy, and money on proposals that you cannot win.
Petty events cannot assume importance regardless of how hard a petty chieftain, warrior, or Hun works to magnify them.	Do not tell your proposal staff that "this is a must win proposal" and then don't give them sufficient resources to prepare a winning proposal.
A chieftain who consistently inspects the work of the warriors and Huns finds that they consistently produce better results.	Top management should take an active part throughout proposal preparation, and not just come in at the last minute with changes.
Huns given tasks without deadlines don't get them done.	Establish reasonable deadlines for proposal draft writing and reviews, and enforce them.
A tribe performs at its best when everyone is assigned the tasks he or she does best for the tribe.	Assign proposal staff that is qualified for the jobs assigned, not just because they are available.

Battle Maxims	Proposal Maxims
A chieftain should stop training his or her warriors and Huns only when winning is no longer important. And I, Attila, King of Huns, am at a loss to fathom when winning may become unimportant for any tribe or for the nation.	Maintain a professional proposal core group and provide them the necessary training to prepare winning proposals. This may require bringing in outside professionals.
Joining tribal efforts in no way diminishes a warrior's or Hun's chance to make a meaningful individual contribution. Rather, joining tribal efforts adds depth and dimension to a meaningful individual contribution.	Make an honest assessment of your strengths and weaknesses, relative to each proposal, and bring in teammates or consultants to strengthen your competitive position.
One of the most insidious ways to abuse power and position is to spend tribal monies irresponsibly.	Don't waste B&P money on proposals that have no chance of winning.
Chieftains create strong morale and discipline in the tribe when they train their warriors and Huns well, tell them what is expected of them, allocate to them the necessary tools and weaponry, and provide them with the leadership required to win.	Top management must fully support every proposal effort, be continually involved, and provide all of the needed resources to complete the job with a winning proposal.
A warrior with high potential is quick to leave a poorly led tribe.	Give your proposal people competent proposal management leadership, or the competent ones will leave and go to work for your competitors.

Well, what do you think? How would you like to compete against Attila The Hun on your next proposal? If you are not willing to compete *against* him, then perhaps you should *follow his advice*.

*How to convince the Government to choose you over
all other offerors—even those with a lower price*

Storyboard Outlining

Storyboard outlining was reputedly invented by the Walt Disney studios to minimize wasted time, effort, and false starts on organizing and preparing their animated cartoon motion pictures. Before computer programming of videos, as many as 50,000 pictures were needed for a full length, animated motion picture. Howard Hughes, active in both movie and aircraft industries, utilized the concept to organize his proposals and avoid false starts in the early 1960s in Hughes Aircraft's *STOP* (Sequential Thematic Organization of Publications) response methodology.

The concept is to outline and review a response section, before writing the section, to ensure that the section meets its requirements, is consistent with the rest of the response, and that authors, book bosses, program managers, and proposal managers are "on the same page."

Storyboard Outlining Preparation

Your Storyboard Outline can be any format that works for you, but it should include the response paragraph number and title, the page budget, author, solicitation references (Section L, M, and SOW/SOO requirements).

To prepare your Storyboard Outline, first study the solicitation requirements for that response paragraph or section and the Solicitation to Response correlation matrix (map of requirements to response) for each response section and paragraph. Then:

- Prepare a bullet chart for that section describing what you plan to write.
- These bullets may be:
  o First sentences for each sub-paragraph.
  o One-line summaries for each sub-paragraph.
  o Just simple thoughts for each sub-paragraph.
- Include conceptual tables, figures, photos, etc.

Don't get into details—the object is just for everyone to understand that the proposed draft complies with the solicitation format requirements, responds to the solicitation program requirements, and fits the overall response approach.

Storyboard Outline Example

The following example shows some of the information that should be shown on the Storyboard Outline Form. For this example we have selected the response paragraph: 3-2.7 Level of Control and Control Methods. The 3- denotes Volume 3, which is the Program Management volume; 3-2. Denotes the Program Management section of Volume 3, and 3-2.7 is the specific response paragraph that addresses this topic. Because there were several different requirements specified in RFP paragraph 8B.3.a, we broke the paragraph down into several separate requirements and added /a, /b, /c, etc. to the paragraph number for computer tracking because computers don't track duplicate paragraph numbers well.

This is the Storyboard heading:

Proposal Paragraph Number: 3-2.7.3
Proposal Paragraph Title: Level of Control and Control Methods
Solicitation Section L: IFPP: Vol. III - Program Management, L-8B.3.a.

The following is the solicitation Section L, Instructions to Offerors from solicitation Section 8, paragraph B.3.a.

Solicitation Instructions: B.3.a. (3) Level of control for performance and design requirements and control methods to be used.

Note that if Section L paragraph B.3.a. had more than one separate requirement, and we needed computer sorting and tracking of RFP paragraph numbers we would add /a, /b, /c, etc. after the RFP paragraph numbers to distinguish among them and still preserve traceability to the RFP paragraphs. Any where you see a /a, /b, /c, etc. you would know that we added that suffix.

The following is from the solicitation Section M, Evaluation Factors for Award:

Section M Factor: M D.3.b3. Management. The management evaluation will be based upon an assessment of the offeror's plan to complete the AWWS full scale development program and ensure that the AWWS is ready for production. Evaluation of this area will be based on the items set forth below. The first item is significantly more important than the other two, which are equal in importance. This is the RFP Section M Evaluation Factors hint at how this response will be evaluated and scored. In this case, it is information only, and there is nothing specific here to address in our response

The following is from the solicitation attachment Statement of Work (SOW):

SOW 3.0 Management/Systems Engineering Objectives: The contractor shall: identify, manage, and mitigate program risks to ensure successful integration, implementation and operation of each AWWS; plan, organize, staff, and oversee the program to deliver the AWWS system on schedule and within cost; and establish the basis for the evolution and/or growth of the baseline system. The contractor will maintain the system configuration and ensure that all version updates to the baseline software that result from further testing, correction of operational failures, or maintenance actions are provided to the Government.

The following shows a requirement to address an issue identified by a competitive assessment of the offeror's strengths and weaknesses. It is a Win Strategy developed from a Brainstorming Meeting that addresses the Soundness of Our Approach to track cost and work performed, identifies the Features of our internal audit system, and emphasizes its Benefits to the Customer.

> S/Mgmt 02: COMPETITION DATABASE: Self Analysis. ISSUE: Milt Cross wants to implement his new internal audit system. [Re: Notes from January 15th Brainstorming Meeting.] CONCERN: Concern is over our ability to track costs and work performed. ACTION: Include a brief discussion of our new internal audit system in our cost management plan, and how we will use it to benefit this program.

The following shows how we will address each SOW task requirement, and will bear in mind the SSEB Assessment Criteria of Understanding the Problem, Compliance with Requirements, and Soundness of Approach.

> Show understanding the problem, compliance with requirements, and soundness of approach to the SOW:
> • Describe how we will identify, manage, and mitigate program risks to ensure successful integration, implementation and operation of each AWWS task.
> • Describe how we will plan, organize, staff, and oversee the program to deliver the AWWS system on schedule and within cost;
> • Explain how our management plan and schedule will deliver the AWWS on time and within budget;
> • Describe program oversight methods and list tracking metrics.
> • Establish the basis for the evolution and/or growth of the baseline system, maintain system configuration, and ensure that all version updates to the baseline software are provided to the Government.
> • Describe how our internal audit system will address and mitigate any risks to the program that could affect cost, schedule, or performance.

Storyboard Outlining Review

The best way to review Storyboard Outlines is to stick whole sections (i.e., Technical, Management, etc.) to the walls. Proposal management "walks the walls," reads the outline out loud, and reviews the various sections for:
- Understanding the requirements,
- Response and compliance with the requirements,
- Soundness of approach,
- Relationships and consistency with related sections,

- Statement(s) of discriminators or themes,
- Whether this topic should be addressed in a different section.

Corrections are noted directly on the Storyboard sheets and initialed by the authors, book bosses, and program and proposal managers.

Here is an example of a Storyboard Outline Form:

Storyboard Outline

Response Para. No.: _____   Author: _____   Page Budget:_____

Response Para. Title.: _____

Section L Para. No.: _____   Section L Para. Title.: _____

Section L - ITO.: _____

_____

Section M Para. No.: _____   Section M Para. Title.: _____

Section M C- Eval. Factor: _____

_____

Response Outline::   Illustration Concept::

_____   _____
_____   _____
_____   _____
_____   _____
_____   _____
_____   _____
_____   _____
_____   _____
_____   _____
_____   _____

Approvals: _____

Implementing Storyboard Outline

Sometimes authors have trouble writing their first drafts from the Storyboard Outlines because they make it too difficult. Actually, it's very simple: to write your first draft from approved outlines:
- Write the first bullet in your new draft.
- Complete that thought.
- Write the next bullet, and so on.

Response RunningStart™

An alternative to Storyboard Outlines is one that Ransone Associates, Inc., developed. This is a continuum process of RFP requirements to Storyboards to Response Draft that eliminates the "start each step with a blank page" disruptions of the traditional Storyboard Outline methods, yet preserves the organizational and communication benefits of the Storyboard Process itself.

RunningStart™ improves first draft quality because it provides all of the RFP response requirements, Storyboard Outlines, and draft preparations in one MS Word file for easy review, revision, and approval. It is especially good for virtual response teams where writers are geographically dispersed. The following illustration shows the format in which:

- The Header identifies the author, supporting authors, page budget, and instructions of completing your draft.
- The response paragraph number and title.
- All solicitation requirements (Section L, ITO, Section M, Evaluation factors for Award, SOW/SOO, etc.
- Special instructions from response management to the authors.
- Space for outlining your response.
- And provisions for preparing your draft after your approach is approved.

This format provides all of the information needed for authors to draft their response, and for reviewers to review their response against the RFP requirements and win strategy themes.

This is only one way of communicating the response requirements and instructions to your authors. Other methods include simple Microsoft Excel spreadsheets with the RFP requirements and response outline listed, with varying levels of details.

Proposal Running Start™

GiantCorp AWWS Proposal

This Proposal Running Start™ form provides a mapping of the RFP requirements that should be considered for addressing in this proposal paragraph. The red font provides the RFP requirements, and the blue font is where you can summarize your approach to addressing these RFP requirements. Proposal management can then review your approach and guide you in writing your proposal draft so that your draft will support the overall proposal approach. The red and blue fonts, as well as this header information, are special MS Word "styles" that can be hidden or redisplayed by the macros embedded in this document.

3-2.7   Level of Control and Control Methods

Instructions to Authors:

Emphasize how our IPTs, with full customer participation, will ensure meeting all cost, schedule, and performance objectives.

IFPP- 8B.3.a. /b   IFPP: Vol III - Program Management

The management proposal must include, but not necessarily be limited to, detailed discussions of the following items: (1) Organizational responsibilities and authority. (2) Control of subcontractors. (3) Level of control for performance and design requirements and control methods to be used. (4) Methods of assurance of program objectives. (5) Control of documentation.

Special Instructions to authors:

M D.3.b. Specific Areas of Evaluation - Management

3. Management. The management evaluation will be based upon an assessment of the offeror's plan to complete the AWWS full scale development program and ensure that the AWWS is ready for production. Evaluation of this area will be based on the items set forth below. The first item is significantly more important than the other two, which are equal in importance: b. ITEM: Proposed Management Controls

Special Instructions to authors:

S/Mgmt 02   COMPETITION DATABASE: Self Analysis

ISSUE: Milt Cross wants to implement his new internal audit system. [Re: Notes from January 15th Brainstorming Meeting.] CONCERN: Concern is over our ability to track costs and work performed. ACTION: Include a brief discussion of our new internal audit system in our cost management plan, and how we will use it to benefit this program.

Special Instructions to authors:

SOO 3.0 MANAGEMENT/SYSTEM ENGINEERING OBJECTIVES

The contractor will: identify, manage, and mitigate program risks to ensure successful integration, implementation and operation of each AWWS; plan, organize, staff, and oversee the program to deliver the AWWS system on schedule and within cost; and establish the basis for the evolution and/or growth of the baseline system. The contractor will maintain the system configuration and ensure that all version updates to the baseline software that result from further testing, correction of operational failures, or maintenance actions are provided to the Government.

Special Instructions to authors:

SOW 1   Test Statement of Work Entry

This is a POW95 development entry. Delete after programming online Proposal Outline development function.

GiantCorp Competitive Sensitive

3-2.7   Level of Control and Control Methods

Instructions to Authors:

Emphasize how our IPTs, with full customer participation, will ensure meeting all cost, schedule, and performance objectives.

Special Instructions to authors:

Outline what you intend to write in this blue font. Use whatever form of outline you like. You may reference other reports or proposals; you may write first sentences, thoughts, or simply ideas; or you may lust list bullet. The idea is to reach an agreement on what you intend to write with the Program and Proposal Managers. It's far better to write your best text now that have to rewrite it the middle of February.

-

After you agree with proposal management on what you will write, draft your proposal below, using the Normal style (black font), responding to the above RFP requirements.

General Response Format

Remember that your response is a sales document, not an engineering document. An engineering/scientific/technical document (down-pointed triangle) has the discussions on top leading to a final conclusion at the bottom. A sales document (response) presents the main sales conclusion at the top (up-pointed triangle) and then reinforces this sale with increasing expansion of proof discussions. The response must generate your customer's desire to select your offer.

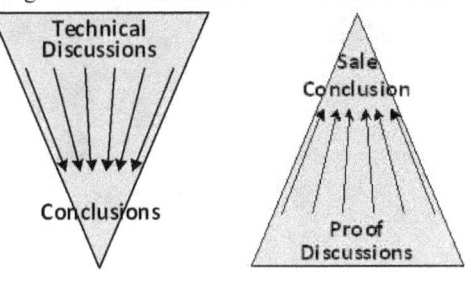

Never forget that your response is not a technical report or a mystery novel—it is a sales document. Make it as easy as possible for the evaluators to find and understand your answers to their questions about your offering. Many evaluators will read just enough to understand what you are offering, and then skip to the next section. Provide this information right up front, like in a newspaper article: who, what, when, and where (the "how much" is restricted to your Cost Volume). In fact, the best response authors are probably journalists.

Write Clear, Effective Responses

Your response must be:
- **CLEAR** or customer will not get the message.
- **WELL ORGANIZED** or she will not find the message.
- **SIMPLE** or he will not understand it.
- **CONCISE** or she will not wade through it.
- **RESPONSIVE** to the RFP or you will appear arrogant.
- **INTERESTING** or he will be bored.
- **CREDIBLE** or she will not believe you.

Why Poor Communicating Occurs

Poor communicating is most likely to occur when the author and the reader have little common background for understanding. To communicate completely, be sure that your readers' backgrounds of understanding are similar to yours—if not, then you must increase that overlap. This Venn Diagram shows how communication can occur only through that overlap.

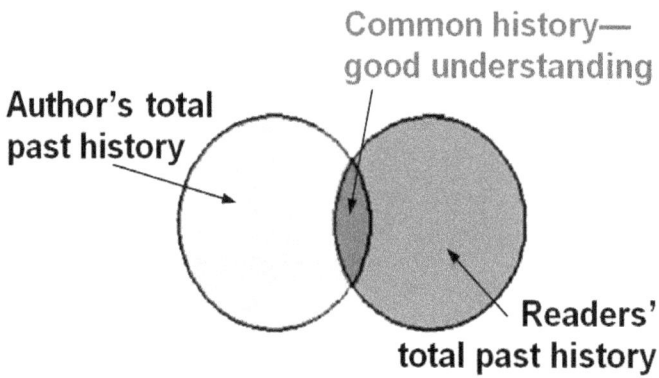

Common history—good understanding

Author's total past history

Readers' total past history

Suppose I tell you that the climate of the UK is maintained relatively mild by the presence of the Atlantic Ocean Gulf Stream. The Stream does this because of its enormous flow rate of 70 sverdrups of warm water. Since you probably don't know what a sverdrup is, this makes no sense to you, and is not convincing. It does not communicate. Now suppose I explain that a sverdrup is equivalent to one million cubic meters per second, or about 264 million U.S. gallons per second. It makes a little more sense, but still you probably cannot comprehend the size of that flow rate.

How to Improve Communicating

Good communicating is most likely to occur when the author and the reader have a large common background for understanding. Now, suppose I explain further that the entire global input of fresh water from rivers to the ocean is equal to about 1 sverdrup, and that the Mississippi River has a flow rate of about 0.002 sverdrups. Suppose I further state that if the water flowing past a point in the ocean for one hour were evaporated, it would take the combined shipping capacity of the entire world to carry the salt. Now can you understand what I'm saying?

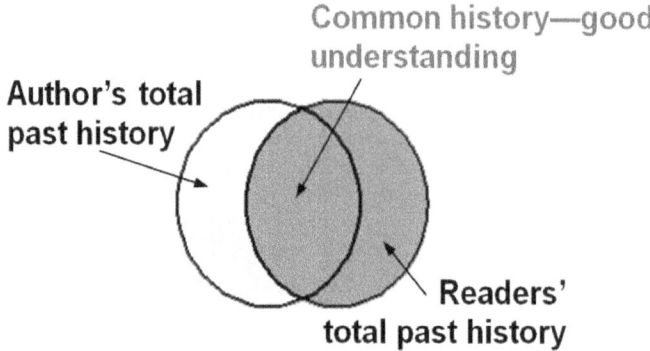

Common history—good understanding

Author's total past history

Readers' total past history

What I have done is expand the overlap between your background and mine. Now we are communicating.

Remember that the evaluators have several responses to read, understand, and score. They can get easily confused about which response is which, especially if you have used many acronyms specific to your own offering. Be sure that they understand your offer by explaining it as clearly and concisely as possible. If you *must* use acronyms, define them in each section, not just the first time you use them, because the evaluators don't read your response sequentially, and may just flip through it searching for answers to their questions. Evaluators don't want to have to look up an acronym list to understand your message.

Communicating Information

We are pretty good at communicating simple ideas and thoughts, but as the subject becomes more complex, we start having trouble communicating.

Simple Communication			Complex Communication
We are good here	**Pretty good here**	**Fair here**	**Poor here**
Routine, habits, automatic reflexes	Explanations, discussions required	Studies, understanding large efforts	New or complex information

Communicating problems occur with technical subjects because they are complex, and we have the most trouble with complex information.

Simplify Your Writing

"Making complicated ideas simple and not misleading is a difficult, time-consuming business. Too many scientists feel that they can't be bothered with the stupid [customer] and must get on with their research. But the best scientists are generally good [communicators]."

Source: Edmund Leach, Psychology Today, July 1974

There is the story of a pupil who asked a noted scientist to explain his point very simply. The scientist studied the blackboard for a while, and then confessed: "I don't understand it well enough to explain it simply."

It is very easy to just state the technical terms. Be sure that the Government evaluators fully understand what you mean.

Complicated Message Must Be Simply Described

The following explanation of a sailboat's sprit-rigged sail was intended to communicate its configuration. What do you think of this description?

"A distinctive characteristic of the barge is its sprit rig. The sprit, known to bargemen as a spreet, was normally a baulk of Oregon or

57

pitch pine, between 11" and 14" in diameter at the heel, and tapering slightly to 9" to 10" at the outer or joggle end. Average length was 30'. Sometimes the sprits were made of steel.

"The heel of the sprit is suspended from the hounds by a wire known as the stanliff, and a collar, called the muzzle, around the mast, just above the tabernacle (mastcase to bargemen) keeps it tight to the mast and enables it to move as the sail is set differently. A tackle from the hounds to a band halfway up the sprit takes the whip from it, and the wire headrope of the sail takes the rest of the weight."

Excerpt from "*The Thames Spritsail Barge*"
by Mike Harper
Cruising World, October, 1977

The jargon in this article is fully understandable to people in the trade, but is gibberish to others. Within a specific discipline, jargon communicates quickly and specifically to others in the trade, so don't disregard it completely. Just be aware that if you want to communicate to others, you must explain it in terms that they understand.

For example if I tell you that an airplane wing has a lift coefficient (C_L) of 1.5 it would be meaningless to you because you don't know what C_L is or whether 1.5 is good, bad, or indifferent. If I explain that C_L is a measure of how much lift the airplane can gain from a specific wing shape, and that 1.5 is about average, you understand more of what I'm telling you.

Readers See What They Expect to See

During training sessions I will project this sentence on a large screen and ask the students to count the "Fs" in the sentence. How many do you see?

FINISHED FILES ARE THE RESULT OF YEARS OF
SCIENTIFIC STUDY COMBINED WITH THE EXPERIENCE
OF MANY YEARS

How many "Fs" do you see now?

FINISHED FILES ARE THE RESULT OF YEARS OF
SCIENTIFIC STUDY COMBINED WITH THE EXPERIENCE
OF MANY YEARS

Now how many "Fs" do you see here?

FINISHED FILES ARE THE RESULT OF YEARS OF
SCIENTIFIC STUDY COMBINED WITH THE EXPERIENCE
OF MANY YEARS

In this case, your eye saw the "Fs" in the words "Of," but your mind skipped over them as being unimportant. Be sure that significant aspects of your story are not presented in words that may be missed.

People Report Only What They Think Is Important

In this experiment with a large audience, I will send three or four people outside the room and then show this slide. If you are familiar with the parlor game *Telephone*, then you understand this exercise.

I would show the slide upside down at first, and then casually correct it. After a few moments I would turn off the slide and invite one of the people into the room from outside, and ask someone in the room to recite exactly what they saw. Then I will invite another from outside, and the first will recite what they were told. The third person was invited back in, and the second would recite what they were told, and so on.

Now, cover the figure so that you can't see it, and, without looking at the figure again, answer the following questions:

- What shape was the figure?
- What was written in the figure?
- Was the first line lower case or upper?
- Was the first line bold or normal font?
- Was the second line upper case or lower?
- Was the second line bold or normal font?
- Was the third line upper case or lower?
- Was the third line bold or normal font?
- Describe the fourth line

The stories usually include most of this information. But the story evolves significantly as each person adds his or her own perspective. I have seen actual pictures of trees appear in the stories, and rectangles, and other details. Few notice that the lower case "a" is repeated. Then I would show the slide again. I would ask the audience whether anyone saw anything different from what the people were relating. No one would mention that the slide was upside down at first. "Didn't anyone see the slide upside down?" "We thought you had just made a mistake." I would remind them that my instructions were to tell "exactly what they saw." This put everyone in the same boat as the people brought in from outside.

Discussions were always enlightening. The consensus was that people repeat *only what they think is important*. That is expected. The big surprise is that if people think something is important, but they don't *know* the information, *then they make it up*! During a response to the US Army to computerize its military health records and make them available worldwide on the Internet, I had to remind my client that one of its teammates, BBN, *had invented the Internet!* This was a huge "gotcha!"

Response Writing Style

Engineers and scientists frequently think that, once they have qualified a statement they don't want to let go of it! They drag it out interminably. Don't try to set a world's record for length—Molly Bloom's soliloquy in the James Joyce novel *Ulysses* contains a sentence of 4,391 words!

Use Short Sentences (long sentences over 20 words make cumbersome reading). Keep Fog Index to about a 12th grade level or less. Do this by keeping sentences as short as possible, and avoid long, multiple syllable words. Use active rather than passive voice: "John Smith, our Program Manager, will provide weekly reports," rather than: "Weekly reports will be provided." Use your customer's name more than your name.

Use the active voice to avoid any ambiguity as to who is doing the job. Write mostly in the first person: "We will…." to be more personal.

Occasionally mix the first and third person to remind the evaluators who you are: "In this section, we explain how GiantCorp will manage your program in order to avoid cost, schedule, or performance problems."

And remember the old adage: KISS: Keep It Short and Simple.

Put benefits before features for a stronger sell than benefits buried in the paragraph after features. This improves your response's "skimmability"

"Higher payload capacities result from eliminating weight from the airframe."

Your customer isn't nearly as interested in saving weight as he/she is in increasing the payload. Weight reduction is a feature, higher payloads is the benefit.

Correct Pace Is Important for Comprehension

There are several good reason why you should consider Pace:
- Reader should understand the material as he or she reads.
- If the Pace is too slow, the reader becomes bored and starts skipping ahead.
- If the Pace is too fast, the reader has to reread the material to understand it.

Set Pace to the Type of Material and the Reader

- If material is familiar and simple—start and maintain a fast pace.
- If material is familiar and complex—start with a fast pace and then slow down.
- If material is unfamiliar but simple—start with a slow pace and then speed up.
- If material is unfamiliar and complex—start and maintain a slow pace.

Pace Controls Comprehension

To Control Pace:

- Speed up pace with longer sentences, longer paragraphs, and fewer graphics.
- Slow down the pace with shorter sentences, shorter paragraphs, bullet charts, and graphics.
- Don't be afraid to write long sentences if the material is simple, easy to understand, or routine.

Avoid "Buzz-Off" Words

Just as there are "buzz" words that we use sometimes, there are "buzz-off" words that we should avoid in a response that is supposed to impress your customer:

These guidelines may seem to be going into too much detail, but the evaluators will judge the quality of your contract work by the example you set in the quality of your

excessive	verify
poor	irregardless
never	time frame
always	perfect
conventional	wonderful
optimize	single up
viable	significant
validate	negligible
"to" as in "spoken to"	inasmuch as
or "write to"	"writer" as in "the
Superlatives	writer feels"
phony "legalese"	

response. Awkward wording is distracting, at best, and a turnoff at worst. Your entire response must convey a professional quality approach.

Misunderstanding Word Meanings Reduces Credibility

Here are some examples of statements made by professionals who should know better.

- Cecil Smith, LA Times TV critic, considered CBS' Bicentennial Minutes: "...singularly unique." *(Unique means "one of a kind," either it's unique or it isn't, there are no qualifications.)*
- Senator Barry Goldwater, commenting on a report that he had condoned organized crime in Arizona: "...not only ridiculous but completely untrue." *(As distinguished from "ridiculous and true?")*
- When asked if it would be premature to discuss new financial arrangement, the NY Times wrote: "...it would be too premature." *(Either it's premature or it isn't.)*

Confirm the meanings of your words through your dictionary—don't use your dictionary just as a spell-checker. Here are some examples of misunderstood words: Many professional news reporters write: "He hoped to obtain some notoriety from his actions." "Notoriety" is bad publicity, not good publicity. Another common mistake is saying: "This component is comprised of..." The word "comprise" means "composed of." The word "unique" means one of a kind, no other like it. It is unique or it isn't. There are no variations of "singularly" or "very" unique.

"Wordiness" is the Most Serious Response Deficiency

In a 1970s survey by a responses consultant, he asked evaluator friends in Air Force, Army, Navy, and NASA what they disliked most about responses, and the unanimous response was "wordiness." This is not the actual number of words in a response, but the use of unnecessary words and phrases. Most adjectives are useless and have no real meaning. "Negligible" and "significant" are two good examples of words with no real meaning. Did you ever read about a cost increase that wasn't "negligible" or an improvement that was not "significant?"

Wordy	Concise
It is my opinion that	I believe
It is quite probable that	Probably
It may be that	Perhaps
I wish to take this occasion to express my thanks	Thank you
Within the course of the next month	Within a month
Please do not hesitate to call me	Call me
Our plan is to set up a procedure to report the status	We will report the status

Source: Sears & Company, Consultants

Professional Writers' Wordiness

Here is a good example of bad writing—it conveys no information. William E. Petersen, in his article *Accommodations For Cruising Boats,* writes:

> "There are many other reasons for today's mediocre cruising boats as compared with yesterday's one-of-a-kind models. Accommodation design problems in today's cruisers are complicated by factors which differ from those of yesteryear combined with new parameters imposed by today's requirements."

Source: *Cruising World*, October, 1977

Overworked Jargon Can Be Used, but With Great Care

We use jargon in our everyday conversations. It can be used in your response, but use it very carefully.

The words "use" and "Utilize" are good examples of how some words can be used well or poorly. They do not mean the same thing.

acronyms	state-of-the-art
"ized" words knowledgeable	unique
Address	interface
authored	develop
feasible	innovative
traceable parameters achievable	novel
proven	use
trade studies	utilize
software	very

Use means, among other things, the act or practice of employing something. Utilize means to turn to practical use or account.

Non-Compliance Benefits

Sometimes you find that you cannot comply with a solicitation requirement. In that case, show how your alternate approach benefits your customer. If the requirement cannot be met by any responder, then you have a powerful case for building in a ghost story about your competitors. More on ghost stories later.

On one proposal, the Navy expected its funding to buy 2520 hours, but at our costs the funding could buy only 1647 hours. Here is our non-compliant response:

> *"The RFP expects to fund 2520 hours, but will actually fund only 1647 hours. Fortunately, we have several applicable and validated computer routines whose 12 hours, plus the 1647 funded hours, will provide data equivalent to your 2520 hours. Additionally, much of the 3500 hours from our Training System Research program is applicable and will increase both the quantity and the quality of the data expected."*

If you cannot comply with any of the RFP requirements, explain why your own approach benefits the Customer. We actually won this contract, even though we were non-compliant with the SOW.

In another case, the RFP specified that the weapons control software must be programmed in the Ada programming language. My clients told me that they could not do this, and when they explained why, I wrote the response:

> *"We understand and fully support your objective in writing the missile control software in Ada, but we cannot do that, and here's why: There is no validated compiler with which to convert the programmer's source code into machine language. Furthermore, there will not be a validated Ada compiler in time to meet your Full Operational Capability schedule. Yes, we know about the New York University compiler, but that is a research compiler, and is not certificated for operational utilization.*
> *"Therefore, in order to meet your FOC schedule, we will program the software upgrade in Fortran 76, and we will build in the Ada characteristics that you need, including Ada's structured, object-oriented composition, modular format, and ease of maintenance."*

Our response made the Competitive Range. I understand that another bidder claimed they would program in Ada, and they were disqualified. Did my ghost story get them eliminated? I can't claim that, but at least it gave the evaluators something to consider.

Avoid Pompous Gobbledygook

Use simple words—don't try to impress. You frequently hear police and firemen on breaking news interviews using these extra words because they sound official, and they have heard others use these words. It just clutters up response text. Use common, straight forward wording that is easy to understand. Consider the following common mistakes and their better translation:

Gobbledygook	English
Limited lane availability	Covered with snow
Activities matrix	Schedule
Will begin executing professional skills	Will begin work
Labor force participation	Work
Quality educational experience	A good education
Met consumer resistance	Didn't sell
Wind energy conversion system	Windmill
A total learning experience	School System
High personal autonomy quotient	Independence, or self-reliance
Total incarceration facility	Jail

Avoid Arrogance

Be careful about how your response might sound to others reading it for the first time. Don't talk down to your customer. There's a wonderful story from the retirement party of Dr. Gaston Foote, minister of the First Methodist Church in Fort Worth, Texas. He was an impressive figure: for his sermon, he turned down all the lights in the sanctuary except for one spotlight on his snow white hair! Someone at his retirement party implied that he lacked humility. Here is his response:

> *I am humble*
> *I am getting humbler all the time*
> *I am proud of my humility*
> *I deserve a lot of credit for my humility because I have so much of which to be proud*
> *Even when I am bragging, I am humble because I am a whole lot better than I say I am*

Be humble, but don't be arrogant with your humility. Don't "talk down" to your customers.

Ghosting & Ghost Busting

Ghost Stories are statements in your response intended to scare your customer about something your competitors may offer. If you suspect that you know what your competitor is going to offer, show a list of your choices including that approach as one of the options you considered. Then explain how you examined each of those choices and rejected them, and show good reasons why you chose your solution over that one.

Equally important to ghosting your competition is "ghost-busting" those scare stories your competitors might say about you. Don't be afraid to be candid:

if your customer doesn't already know about the skeletons in your closet, you can bet that your competitors will enlighten him. Acknowledge your past mistakes, and explain why that won't happen again. Admission of weakness is not weakness—it is strength, because the next time you brag, your customer will be more inclined to believe you.

War Story:
On one proposal, my client admitted that on a previous contract they had difficulties with their data item deliveries. They were late and their format made them useless to the Government. They didn't want to mentions this. Upon questioning, however, I discovered that they had followed the Data Item instructions exactly, but the prescribed format was wrong. They worked with the Government Program Manager and resolved the problem, which resulted in a commendation to the Program Manager. Powerful stuff that we put in the proposal management section!

Data Delivery and Transmittal Paragraph

Original paragraph:

"Instructions for data delivery and transmittal have been examined. Compliance, without exception, is to be adhered to in our submittal of data."

Revised paragraph:

"We will deliver and transmit the data in full compliance with your instructions."

Don't be afraid to commit yourself to compliance with RFP requirements. Someone, long ago, used to writing lofty military reports, wrote the opening sentence to his Letter of Transmittal with the following words;

"GiantCorp is pleased to submit our……"

This is a bald-faced lie! No company is "pleased" to work their tails off trying to figure out what the customer wants and writing a response within the strict dictates of the solicitation Instructions to Offers! Here is a much better opening paragraph that shows our enthusiasm for the program:

"(GiantCorp) is proud to submit our fully compliant proposal for the Tactical Data Network and the Digital Tech Control, in response to your solicitation M67854-98-R-2089. We share the Corp's vision for improved, economical tactical communications with growth capability to easily accommodate emerging technologies. We assure you of our corporate commitment to the success of the TDN/DTC program."

Use Fog Index and Pace to make your responses easy to read and understand

If you want to help your evaluators read and understand your responses without creating any confusion or misunderstanding, you must write them to be easy to read and understand. As Thomas Hood, humorist, poet, and essayist, wrote to the London periodical *The Athenaeum* in 1837: "easy reading is damned hard writing!" Fortunately there are two techniques that can help you, Fog Index and Pace.

The Flesch Fog Index roughly equals the years of schooling in that subject. For example, Harpers Magazine has a Fog index of about 10.9, Reader's Digest about 7, and Military Manuals about 3-4. There is a formula for calculating Fog Index that utilizes the average number of words per sentence and how many big (polysyllable—more than three syllables) words are in the text.

$$\text{Fog Index} = 0.4 \text{ x (WPS + PSW)}$$

Where:

WPS is the average number of words per sentence
PSW is the number of words of 3 syllables or more per 100
words
0.4 is a sizing factor to match the Fog Index to years of schooling

Ignore proper nouns, combinations of short words, and suffixed words. A Fog Index less than 12 is difficult because of the many polysyllable words in technical writing. It would result in too many short, choppy sentences. Also, it is questionable whether many long, technical words should really be counted if they are in the common, technical vocabulary of the disciplines you are addressing. But note that many people will likely read your response, many of them ignorant of words common to specific vocations.

Here are some examples: The first is the original RFP wording:

> *"The logistic support system for the V/STOL Type A Weapon System will be a critical factor in its successful deployment and utilization. NAVAIR places a priority on logistic considerations in all efforts related to developing this system. Wide geographical dispersion of limited numbers of aircraft may require major revisions to the application of the Naval Aviation Maintenance Program and current Logistic Support Policy. Accordingly, it is the intent to solicit innovative approaches that may be used to enhance the eventual Integrated Logistic Support (ILS) program strategy. However, such approaches must be presented in sufficient detail to permit informed analysis."*
>
>

5 sentence s
99 word s
21 polysyllable word s
Fog Index = 16.

We can't do anything about Fog Index in RFPs, which sometimes makes them difficult to understand. The following is a possible revision to the text to make it easier to read and easier to understand:

> *"The logistic support system for the Type A V/STOL Weapon System will be a critical factor in the use of the weapon system. NAVAIR requires logistic considerations in all parts of this system. Major changes to the use of the Naval Aviation Maintenance Program and current Logistic Support policy may be needed because of the wide dispersion of small numbers of aircraft. Give us your new ideas for Integrated Logistic Support (ILS) in enough detail for a complete evaluation."*
>
> *4 sentence s*
> *79 word s*
> *6 polysyllable word s*
> *Fog Index = 11. 2*

This version would be much easier to understand and is a 20% reduction in word count.

Here is an example with both high Fog Index and too fast a Pace:

> *"Engine to engine comparisons were then developed using configuration 7. Figure 1-128 shows the takeoff gross weight (TOGW) of each candidate engine/configuration 7 combination for aircraft concept B (see Figure 0176 in Section 1.1) normalized to the TOGW of the JT15D-5 combination. Concepts A and B were considered to be identical insofar as the sizing process was concerned. Ranked in order of TOGW the LARZAC engine required an increase in TOGW of 4% over the JT15D-5 powered configuration. The TFE 731-2 required 5% and the TFE 731-3 required 6%. The scaled GE27/F1(A1) resulted in a reduction of 14% but, since it is a paper engine, it was not considered as a realistic contender for the best of the existing engines on the basis of TOGW. The same relative ranking of the engines held for concept C, so JT15D-5 powered versions of configuration 7 were used for Aircraft A, B and C."*

This was the original paragraph in a GiantCorp response. It is very confusing, and has to be reread in order to understand the message. Fog Index is slightly high at 13.3, but "pace" is much too fast because of the rapid presentation of data, references, and numbers.

The following shows the draft corrected for both Fog Index and Pace:

> *"Use of the JT15D-5 engines resulted in the lightest TOGW for the configuration 7 baseline aircraft, as shown in Figure 1-128. This result is valid for all three aircraft concepts with respect to approach speed and flying qualities. The TOGW would be 4% heavier with the LARZAC engines, 5% heavier with the TFE 731-2, and 6% heavier with the TFE 731-3. Scaled GE27/F1 (Al) engines would have reduced TOGW 14% but they were rejected because they are just "study" engines.*

Fog Index is reduced to 10.4, and comprehension is greatly improved because pace is correct for the material being presented. Fog Index is improved by 22%, and word count is reduced from 148 to 78, a 47% reduction!

The Plumber Anecdote

To illustrate further, the story goes that a plumber with a rather limited command of English wrote the Bureau of Standards in Washington. You may be familiar with this anecdote. It is a good example of the wording trap in which officials sometimes find themselves because they believe that this is the way they should talk to sound authoritative.

The plumber wrote that he found that hydrochloric acid opened clogged drainage pipes in a hurry and wanted to know if it was a good thing to use.

A bureau scientist wrote him back: "The efficacy of hydrochloric acid is indisputable, but the corrosive residue is incompatible with metallic permanence." (Fog Index = 26.4).

The plumber promptly wrote back thanking the scientist for telling him the method was all right. The scientist showed the letter to his boss, who got worried. "We cannot assume," he wrote the plumber, "responsibility for the production of toxic and noxious residue with hydrochloric acid and suggest you use an alternative procedure." (Fog Index = 22.4).

The plumber, figuring somebody up there in the Bureau of Standards really liked him, promptly replied that the acid was working just dandy.

This letter was passed on to the section Head, who broke off the correspondence tersely:

"Don't use hydrochloric acid! It eats the hell out of the pipes!"
(Fog Index 5.6).

No one can misunderstand this message—simple and to the point.

Another point: always use your online spellchecker—but don't rely on it completely, and watch out for your word processor's automatic spelling corrections.   It can embarrass, and it will!

Ode to the Spell Checker

Eye halve a spelling chequer
It came with my pea sea
It plainly marquees four my revue
Miss steaks eye kin knot sea.
Eye strike a key and type a word
And weight four it two say
Weather eye am wrong oar write
It shows me strait a weigh.
As soon as a mist ache is maid
It nose bee fore two long
And eye can put the error rite
Its rare lea ever wrong.
Eye have run this poem threw it
I am shore your pleased two no
Its letter perfect awl the weigh
My chequer tolled me sew.

68

My spell checker had no problems with this poem.

Always, *always* proofread your draft carefully, and look for individual words, not just skimming through it. Your eye sees what it expects to see, and will fool your brain into thinking everything is OK. Try reading the following. You will be amazed that you can read this gibberish easily.

> *Aoccdrnig to a rscheearch at Cmabrigde Uinervtisy, it deosn't mttaer in what oredr the ltteers in a wrod are, the olny iprmoetnt tihng is taht the frist and lsat ltteer be at the rghit pclae. The rset can be a total mses and you can sitll raed it wouthit porbelm. Tihs is bcuseae the huamn mnid deos not raed ervey lteter by istlef, but the wrod as a wlohe. Smilpy amzanig huh?*

This is why typos escape your corrections. To clearly see typos, read your text backwards. (By the way: This paragraph drove my spellchecker nuts!)

Importance of Graphics

Years ago at a Toastmasters International meeting I conducted an experiment to evaluate the effectiveness of graphics in communicating information. I read a report of California traffic statistics. In the first third I just read the numbers. In the second third I repeated the numbers for emphasis. In the last third I showed a chart. Then I handed out a pop-quiz! This shows the percent of correct answers for each section.

- Where I just read the material, retention was 26%.
- Where material is explained, retention was 34%.
- Where I showed a chart, retention was 86%.

These numbers are very close to other similar experiments.

> **War Story:**
> *At the Air Force Flight Test Center, Edwards AFB, California, where I was a flight test project engineer in the early 1960s, I had to brief the commanding general on the importance of Vertical Takeoff and Landing Aircraft to our mission. I was told I had two hours for the "flip chart" presentation. The general was an hour late. Bob White was flying the X-15 to 250,000 feet to earn his astronauts wings, and the general was running to the window to look for him. The night before, a sergeant had been killed at a railroad crossing with another sergeant's wife, and the sergeant's mother called three times to talk with the general. These were the conditions under which I was giving this important briefing! But I was ready: When I got to the last chart, I looked him right in the eye, and said: "general, if I only had two minutes of your time, this is the one chart I would show you." I had his undivided attention for two minutes, and two weeks late he stated that information in a speech to the local Chamber of Commerce.*

Importance of Color in Graphics

Studies have verified the importance of color in graphic illustrations:

- Color increases retention by 18%.
- Color raises a prospect's readiness to buy by 26%.
- Color boosts readership of a memo (or response) by 41%.

I don't know the source of these statistics, but I believe the trend is reasonable.

Response Graphics (pictures, charts, tables, graphs, etc.)

Responses should have about 50/50 graphics and text. The graphics should be simple, easy to read, and understandable within 10 seconds. They should complement or supplement the text, and have a descriptive title and an action caption. The action captions should name the illustration and relate features to benefits, but be careful not to claim benefits that the illustration doesn't support.

Here is an example of an action caption that identifies the illustration number, its title, and its benefit:

> *Figure 12. VENDOR CORRECTIVE ACTION REQUEST (VCAR) PROCESS corrects and documents any non-conformance*

Don't waste words explaining your illustrations in the text. Your illustrations should carry the message, and your text should elaborate the details. A picture should be worth a thousand words (but it takes a thousand times the memory, according to some computer wags).

Response Graphics

- Effective use of color, white space, and design can make your graphics more effective.
- Graphics should be sized, spaced, and located so that they can be seen while the evaluator is reading the relevant body text.
- Avoid landscape graphics because they require the reader to turn the document.
- Graphics (flow charts, etc.) should flow from top left to bottom right.

Response Graphics Numbering

Authors frequently create large, complicated illustrations numbering schemes, including the volume and paragraph number, and use a separate numbering sequence for tables and other graphics. This is cumbersome and confusing, creates unnecessary problems in renumbering when the illustration is moved to another paragraph, or the paragraph number changes. Don't do this. Also, use only one numbering sequence for all of your illustrations: tables, flow-charts, organization charts, photos, whatever!

Authors should obtain a Graphics number from the Response Coordinator, which should be a simple sequence number, based upon when it was logged, and perhaps a prefix with the volume number or author's initials. This number should be put on the graphic and becomes a permanent reference for that illustration. This figure number in your text and figure caption avoids changing the number every time the figure is moved or the paragraph number changes. Don't be alarmed that the first figure may be Figure 325 and the second figure may be Figure 12. The number is only to tie the illustration to its text reference. Your Pubs Department or Coordinator will renumber the figures at book-makeup just before publication.

> **War Story:**
> *On one response, where we had a two week late start and I was the coordinator as well as the response manager (not good!) I asked the authors to set up their own illustrations numbering system, which comprised their initial plus a simple sequence number for their figures. This worked fine.*

Graphics Should Stand Alone

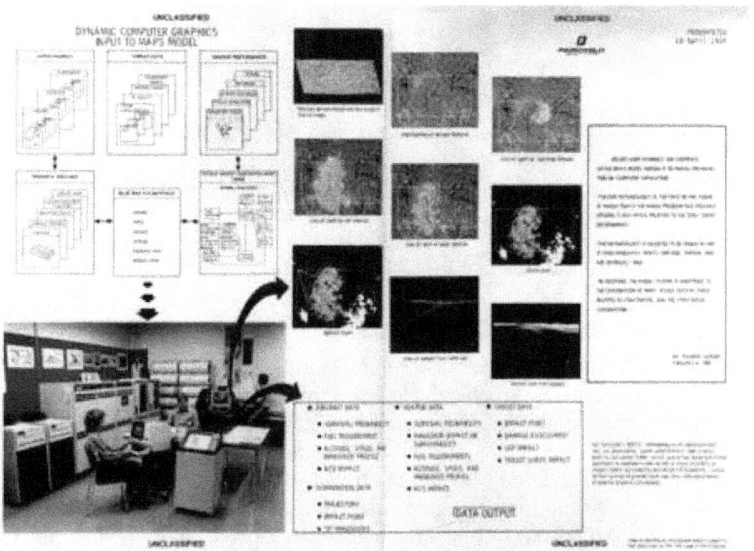

This illustration for a cruise missile response shows the real-time simulation of a mission. The upper left describes the output, the photograph shows the company computer room, the terrain photos show what the missile would "see' during its flight with known hostile anti-missile batteries, the table at the bottom shows the data that is output, and the figure on the right margin is a testimonial from a USAF Avionics Lab scientist. The paragraph in the lower right hand corner is the action caption.

Graphics Should Tell the Story

On one proposal I was so impressed with the character and dedication of the workers, that I had the company photographer photograph them during each step of the manufacturing process. He also got quotations from each, such as: "Shirley Dodson records Strand Burn Test Data. She is Senior Test Technician, and has been with (GiantCorp) 40 years." I also showed a normal flow chart across the bottom, but showing the actual people was a big plus in our Quality Section, and contributed to our big win. This is an 11 x 17 foldout, well worth its two-page count.

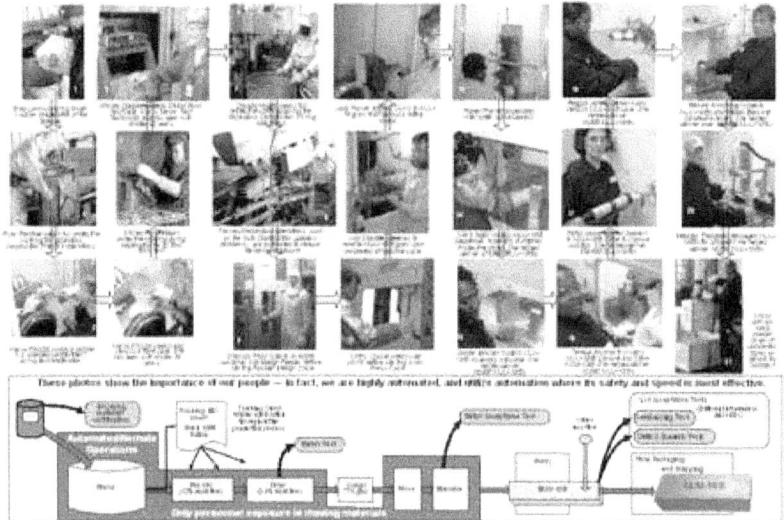

Importance of Graphics Quality

Don't skimp on the quality of your illustrations. People are used to the high quality of advertising graphics, and know the capabilities of modern desktop publishing and PowerPoint presentations. They may judge the quality of your potential work by the quality of your illustrations. Professional graphics artists are worth their cost, and don't be mislead by a high hourly cost—they can produce beautiful, convincing graphics in a fraction of the time your authors can. Your authors are better utilized in creating your response, not in laboring over illustrations details. This is not to say that your authors shouldn't prepare their own tables, and simple figures, but leave the more complex illustrations to the professionals.

The following is an example of an author's draft illustration and the professional version put into the proposal.

72

Graphics Input	Graphics Output (The 24Hour Company)

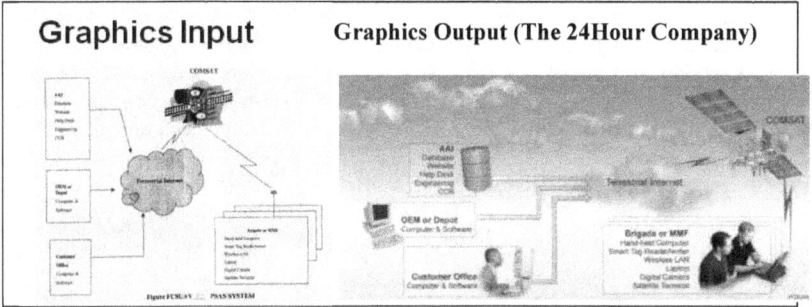

RFPs usually disclaim the desire for fancy embellishments. This is true if the frills get in the way of your message, but you want a nice looking document, and the evaluators appreciate nice illustrations and formatting. The 24 Hour Company in Falls Church, Virginia, does a terrific job with illustrations.

Eye-Catching Covers

You want your cover to shout: "read me first!" so that your response will be the standard against which the others are judged.

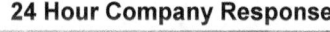

Author's Input	24 Hour Company Response

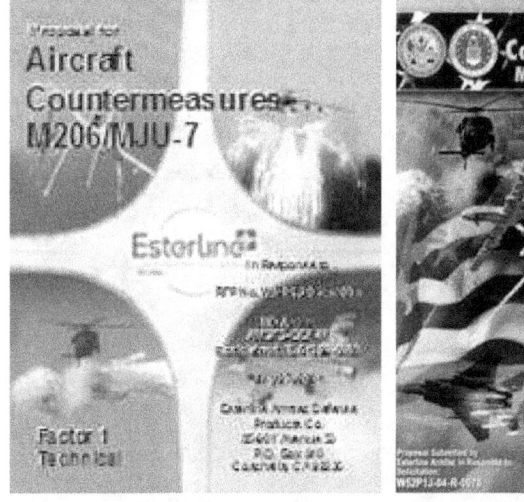 

This new cover cries "Read me first!" and was well worth its $1,100 cost.

Cover Letter—Direct Contact with the Source Selection Authority

A survey done years ago of Department of Defense and NASA Source Selection Authorities discovered that SSA's always read the cover letters and

Executive Summaries. This is your chance to talk directly to the individual who has final authority in giving you the contract. Don't blow this opportunity! Don't waste precious response space and SSA time with obvious, mundane trivia. Get right to the point, showing your capability and enthusiasm for this program, major features and benefits, and concern for delivering a risk-free accomplishment for the SSA's career.

Mrs. *Colonel* SSA wants to retire as Mrs. *General* SSA, and if that doesn't happen, retired *Colonel* SSA will have a most unpleasant retirement!

The following opening paragraph is ho hum! A waste of words because it states the obvious:

> ***Original, wordy, opening paragraph:***
> *"In response to the Naval Air Development Center RFP Solicitation Number N62269-R-0468, GiantCorp proposes to conduct a conceptual study of Advanced Navy Jet Trainer Aircraft. This response describes the character of the study effort. We have the necessary resources to accomplish this study and have developed a plan that is responsive to every aspect of the RFP."*

Your cover letter will be read, not only by the SSA, but by many others, so it should make the first good impression. If it gets off to a bad start, your response will have a hard time overcoming it.

> ***Revised, enthusiastic opening paragraph:***
> *"GiantCorp has assembled a top team of Naval aircraft designers and undergraduate pilot training experts and is eager to conduct a conceptual study of the Advanced Navy Jet Trainer Aircraft. This response describes our plan for the study, shows that we have all of the resources necessary, and is fully responsive to the RFP."*

My re-write expresses our enthusiasm for the program, gives some credibility to our training plan approach, and states that we understand and will be fully compliant and responsive to the RFP requirements.

Executive Summary

Although not scored, the Executive Summary is very influential and is *always read* by the Source Selection Authority, as well as by the evaluators. If the Executive Summary has a weak sell, your customer may not read the rest of the response, and even if it is read, they will be looking for reasons to eliminate you. The Executive Summary should follow and answer the concerns of the RFP Section M Evaluation Factors for Award because that RFP section lists your customer's main concerns. You should also have been "working the customer" long in advance, and know what he/she wants that might not be expressed in the solicitation. Address these in your Executive Summary, also.

On any solicitation, your customer may have many responses to evaluate in a very short time. It is likely that they will make a tentative decision from the Executive Summary, and skim the detailed responses only to justify their selection or rejection. Therefore, your Executive Summary must:

- Follow the RFP Section M Evaluation Factors for Award.
- Address the customer's concerns and desires and show your understanding of those concerns and desires.
- Be specific about what you offer.
- Emphasize the unique features of your offer (technical, management, cost) and their benefits to cost, schedule, or performance.
- Show how your solution is lowest risk and lowest cost and why you believe it is the best value.

Section Headlines

Section and paragraph headlines are effective ways of communicating your story quickly to the skimming readers, and are short paragraphs just below the section or paragraph titles. They should summarize and be fully substantiated by the following text, and convey your major win theme for that topic. They should be simple, factual statements that connote compliance, discriminators, and low risk, summarize the section or paragraphs, and set the tone for the following section or paragraph. They must state credible factual information, be substantiated in the following write up, and make good first impressions to the skimming readers. Set them apart by special formatting, such as boxed text or italics.

Here is an example of a good section headline:

> *"We will use the same manufacturing and test facilities, TDP, equipment, and people to produce your new M206 and MJU-7 decoy flares, in a seamless transition, from our existing M206 and MJU-7 production facility in which we have produced over 2 million flares."*

Response Section Introductions

If you can spare the page budget, you should consider writing an introduction at the front of each major section or subsection. These should be mini-executive summaries of the sections or subsections that follow. They should summarize the section or subsection and contain all of your themes and discriminators discussed in the text. Main themes, discriminators, and features-benefits should flow down from the Executive Summary to Section Introductions to the Subsection Introductions. They should be factual, concise, address the evaluation criteria for award, and be clearly written for the skimming reader.

Oral Responses

The government has been "burned" many times when a contractor's Program Manager knew little about the program he/she was to manage because the response was written by outside consultants. On one proposal there were 12 of us consultants writing the proposal. On another major proposal for a US Air Force primary trainer aircraft virtually no one who wrote the proposal was still at the company upon contract award. As a result, many solicitations require an oral presentation. This may supplement written submission or be the sole response submission.

Orals are usually presented by a limited contractor attendance with no outside help, sometimes only by the Program Manager. These are a special type of response that may or may not also include extensive hard copy or electronic copies. Microsoft PowerPoint slides are usually projected, and will be submitted in advance on or before the response submission time and date. The contractor may present only the pre-submitted material, but may elaborate orally to clarify the subject or explain any deficiencies. Time is limited for the formal presentation, and a question and answer period usually follows.

Oral presentations usually are not scored, but will be considered in the overall evaluation.

Oral Response Planning

Your oral response should be carefully planned and prepared, not just "hey, stand up there and tell them about our wonderful ideas!" You should determine from the Response Manager who will be in charge of the Oral Presentation, who will develop the Orals slides (i.e., individual authors, graphics illustrators under the supervision of the authors, a separate Orals team), who will produce the Orals slides (the response production team, or a separate graphics group), who will rehearse the Orals presenters, and who will travel to present the Orals to the customer.

Orals Response Preparation

Follow the solicitation format, time limit, and content instructions to the letter, if provided. Slides should provide an Executive Summary, Technical, Management, and other sections as specified in the solicitation. Keep the slides simple–provide details in the slide notes and in your oral remarks. As for font size, you should be able to read your slides easily if you drop them on the floor.

Orals should be rehearsed several times before presenting, and the use of a video camera will identify serious as well as annoying problems with your slides and with your delivery.

Any other company attendees (these are usually severely restricted) should monitor your timing so that you can present all of the material in the time allotted. Practice hand signals for "speeding up," "slowing down," and "cut it off!"

PART VII – RISK ASSESSMENT AND MITIGATION

How to convince your customer that his/her career is
safer with your Risk Management Plan
than with your competitors'

Note that your risk management plan in not just to mitigate any risks to the program, it's mostly to mitigate any *risks to the SSA's career*. You *must* identify any cost, schedule, or performance risks of your offering using this matrix. This includes not just the risks *you think* might occur, but the risks that *your customer is concerned about*. The Impact should be relatively easy to assess, but the Probability of Occurrence may be just a guess. Try to make an assessment that will be acceptable to your customer, and one that you can further justify if necessary. Explain your assessment in your response, don't just state the risk level.

Occurrence	Negligible No effect on program	Minor Small cost/ sched. increase	Moderate Moderate, some reqts. not met	Serious Major, min. reqts. Not met	Critical Program failure
1-10% Very unlikely	Low risk	Low risk	Low risk	Moderate Risk	Moderate Risk
11-40% Unlikely	Low risk	Low risk	Moderate Risk	Moderate Risk	High Risk
41-60% Half the time	Low risk	Moderate Risk	Moderate Risk	Moderate Risk	High Risk
61-90% Likely	Moderate Risk	Moderate Risk	Moderate Risk	High Risk	High Risk
91-100% Very likely	Moderate Risk	High Risk	High Risk	High Risk	High Risk

The following tables offer suggestions on how to identify your risk levels. Basically they help you assess the development and production state of your offering by assessing the complexity of your offering and how much you have progressed in your development.

Design Risk Assessment

You can use these design risk definitions in your text to explain your risk assessment. This will show your Understanding of the Requirements and

Soundness of Approach to the Government evaluators. These tables also show possible risk mitigation actions and suggest work completed or to be completed that lowers the risks. High risk is level 5.

Complexity

1. Minor modification of existing system	2. Moderate modification of existing system	3.Significant modification of existing system	4. Major modification of existing system	5.Innovative, complex, new design

Concept

1. Minor mod. of fully developed design that meets reqmt.	2. Moderate modification of an existing concept, data are available showing compliance with reqmt.	3. Similar concept exists on another program, able to meet reqmt. by analysis	4. Proof of concept has been demonstrated	5. New concept, requires significant development

Hardware Complexity

1. Simple design with minor complexity	2. Moderate increase in complexity	3. Significant increase in complexity	4. Major increase in complexity	5. Extremely complex

Hardware Maturity

1. Existing: minor redesign	2. Existing: moderate redesign	3. Significant change, but feasible	4. Technology available, complex design	5. State-of-the-art, some research complete

Materials Maturity

1. Materials used in existing system	2. Real part testing with durability and supportability data available	3. Complex prototype testing completed	4. New material with some test experience	5. Materials not completely identified

Parts and Materials Selection

1. Parts and materials operate well below the allowable thermal and/or mechanical stress levels	2. Parts and materials operate slightly below the allowable thermal and/or mechanical stress levels	3. Parts and materials operate at the allowable thermal and/or mechanical stress levels	4. Parts and materials operate slightly above the allowable thermal and/or mechanical stress levels	5. Parts and materials operate above the allowable thermal and/or mechanical stress levels

Production Process

1. Producibility of design demonstrated at full rate production	2. Producibility of design demonstrated on pilot production run	3. Producibility of design demonstrated on a prototype	4. Manufacturing and supportability have input in design phase and sign production drawings	5. Manufacturing and supportability sign production drawings completed

Weight Prediction

1.Actual design weight known, off-the-shelf	2. Design complete, actual material weight is known	3. Estimates based on mix of analysis and known material weights	4. Estimates based on analytical models, materials are known	5. Estimates based on analysis only

Risk Mitigation Plan

Your risk mitigation plan should identify the risk, its risk level, your closure schedule, and your metrics for monitoring progress and completion.

	Mgmt Risk #1	Tech Risk #1
Risk Summary	Carrying case teammate undecided	Awaiting customer definition of duty cycle
Prob. of Occur	41-50%	61-90%
Impact	Moderate	Serious
Risk Level	Moderate (M)	High (H)
Risk Mitigation	Backup teammate identified, would cost 5% more	Work with customer to expedite finalization
Closure Criteria	Backup teammate certified by our QC and contract signed	Customer signoff on duty cycle
Closure Date	2/10/2016	2/10/2016

Risk Watch List

Some activities might not appear to have risks at this time, but they could impact the program should they occur. This also includes things that the Customer thinks are risky but you don't. Identify them and put them on a "watch list" and include a statement such as:

> "We do not foresee any problems at this time because they have a low probability of occurring, but they have the potential of impacting the program should they occur. Therefore, we are placing them on our watch list, and will monitor the metrics that track their likelihood of occurring."

You must define some metric that would alert you if there is some concern over meeting your cost, schedule, or performance requirements, and track that metric, reporting to the Customer. If the risk materializes, then you must formulate a risk mitigation plan and implement it.

Risk Reduction "Waterfall" Chart

For high risks, you should provide a risk reduction "waterfall" chart against which your customer can measure your progress to risk mitigation. Note that this risk is common to all bidders because it is created by your customer. Don't be shy about bringing these risks to your customer's attention because they are inherent risks to all, over which you have no control, and you should not be held accountable. This is a potential ghost story.

The following example is for *Technical Risk # 1, Awaiting customer definition of duty cycle*:

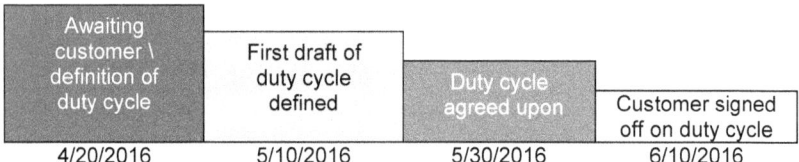

Awaiting customer \ definition of duty cycle	First draft of duty cycle defined	Duty cycle agreed upon	Customer signed off on duty cycle
4/20/2016	5/10/2016	5/30/2016	6/10/2016

Risk Identification and Mitigation Process

It's not enough to identify the perceived risks and your plan to mitigate them. You must also define the process you will use to implement that plan. Your plan must be proactive, involve your customer, identify the risks to cost, schedule, or performance, and prove that your plan will mitigate those risks. The following is a suggested process that I have used successfully many times. It may be customized to accommodate Integrated Product Teams.

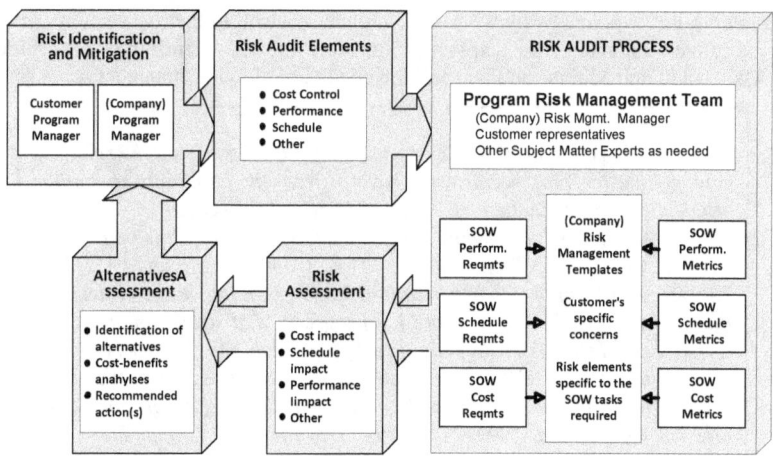

A Contracting Officer's Letter

The following is from the Government Contracting Officer's letter to GiantCorp announcing that our response lost for *Development and Formulation of a Computerized Modular Missile Life Cycle Cost Model, (June, 1980).* The Response Manager didn't want to scare the customer, and downplayed the difficulties and risk inherent in developing the Cost Estimation Relationships (CERs) required by the RFP. This assessment is exactly right!

War Story:
(a)   *Understanding the Problem (failure to understand).*
"While the response shows some evidence of knowledge and experience in the development of cost estimating techniques, your experience does not appear to be extensive with no examples given for modeling the RDT&E process. You present a limited and inadequate description of how you intend to use this. A very general discussion on in-house design/cost/performance trades is provided on pp 14-15 but your Aircraft Synthesis Analysis Program and Missile Integrated Design Analysis System are broad brushed and not specifically detailed as required by the Technical Evaluation Criteria. You cite no particular difficulties associated with the required effort except in the data acquisition area. This shows lack of understanding of the problem since difficulty is inherent when addressing the wide spectrum of missiles that are covered in the SOW."

Cover Letter Risk Statement

In the following cover letter for GiantCorp's response to develop a digital communication system to the US Marine Corps, we acknowledged the risks, predominantly caused by having to interface with existing communication systems, but explained why we had them under control. In the risk section of the Executive Summary we explained in more detail, identifying our Risk Assessment and Mitigation Plan, and included the following statement:

War Story:

*"TDN / DTC is not a risk free program, but we are convinced the risks are manageable for [us] because we have proven our capability in similar programs. These include the AN/TTC-38, AN/TTC-39, AN/TYC-39, Mobile Subscriber Equipment (MSE), Improved MSE for Taiwan (IMSE), CHS-2, AN/TTC-56, Tactical Secure Data Communications (TASDAC), Theater Deployable Communications, and Leading Edge Advanced Package (TDC/LEAP). These are not programs that stretch the point for relevance to TDN/DTC; they are directly applicable to the tasks at hand. In most instances, TDN/DTC must interface with these systems. We are so confident in our ability to furnish a technically superior solution to the Marine Corps that [we] **guarantee** that our TDN and DTC will interoperate with all current DoD communications equipments."*

In our cover letter we also included a small map that showed that we were on the same coast and same time zone as our customer, implying that our competitor, on the opposite coast and three time zones away, would be less available or responsive to customer communications.

We won his contract by a wide margin!

PART VIII – INTEGRATED PROGRAM MANAGEMENT

*Why it's important and how to prepare it with
a common numbering scheme*

Integrated Program Management (IPM)–Why it is Needed

The Government got tired of trying to monitor programs using only long interval milestones, with no idea of whether the Contractor would meet them until it was too late. This was caused by a lack of tracking between the Contract Work Breakdown Structure (CSOW) and the Master Schedule, lack of information for sound go-ahead decisions, and premature implementation of next phases. This resulted in failure to meet requirements, costly and time consuming re-work, program delays, and cost overruns—not good for the Source Selection Authority's career.

IPM provides a management tool that corrects these problems by establishing "inch stones" or "pebbles" along the way with which to monitor progress, and verifiable criteria that enables the government to proceed with confidence.

These criteria provide specific program assignments for accountability, program reviews with specific requirements to be met before government approval to enter the next—usually more costly—phases, specific tracking of detailed, measurable Contract Statement of Work (CSOW) accomplishments against the Contract Work Breakdown Structure (CWBS), and the approved program schedule.

This is accomplished by Integrated Project/Process Teams (IPTs) responsible for specific CSOW elements, CSOW tracked directly to the CWBS, and Program Reviews (Events) to approve funding for each subsequent program phase, with measurable CSOW accomplishment and entry and exit criteria. The detailed CSOW accomplishments are defined in the Integrated Master Plan (IMP), and the program is managed IAW the Integrated Master Schedule (IMS).

Detailed instructions may be found in *Air Force Materiel Command's Integrated Master Plan/Integrated Master Schedule (IMP/IMS) Guide, Prepared for AFMC Acquisition Center of Excellence, by RHT, INC. through VERIDIAN, AFMC 03-128,* Authored by James L. DeStout and K. Richard Cosgrove. (Incidentally, I have discussed my specific approach with Jim DeStout and he agrees that my approach is fine.)

Principles of IPM

The principles of IPM follow the criteria for a good newspaper story, by defining who, what, how, when, where, and how much.
- IPT – defines **who** will do the work.
- IMP – defines **what** CSOW work will be accomplished.
- CSOW – defines **how** the work will be done.

- IMS – defines **when** and **where** the work will be done, and the details and sequencing of how it will be done.
- CWBS – defines **how much** the work costs and **how it will be invoiced.**

This concept provides a cohesive, management process for meeting all cost, schedule, and performance contractual goals.

The Integrated Project/Product Team (IPT) Concept

The IPT concept is simple in principle but sometimes difficult to implement. In this concept, the people most involved with a product or component have full decision responsibility for its success because they know best the detailed work to be accomplished and what it will take to do the jobs. The difficulty comes when middle managers believe their authority is being usurped by their subordinates.

This Venn diagram representation of an IPT can be used in your proposal:

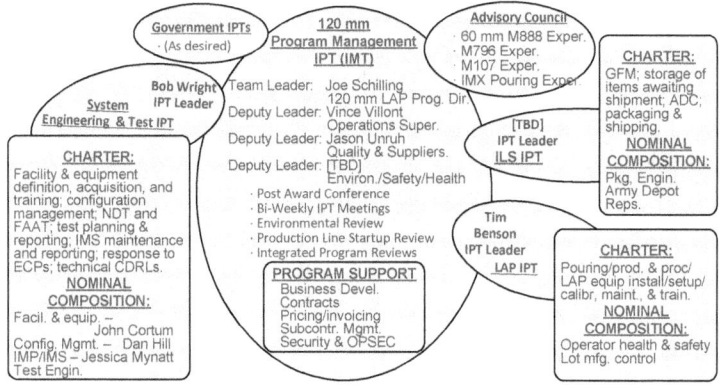

The Venn diagram overlaps show that the Sub-IPT leaders (i.e., SET-IPT, ILS-IPT, etc.) are members of the Program Management IPT. It also shows the Government IPTs participation.

I like to show an Advisory Council that shows how the company's past experience is actually integrated with program management to benefit the program from Lessons Learned on similar, past programs. Companies always tout their past experience, but this past experience *does not reside with the company*, but *with the individuals who did the actual work*! And frequently these individuals are not working this program—they are busy with the contract they won! The Advisory Council is free, it is not charged to the contract, but is covered in the company overhead. These are experts from related programs or people recognized and respected by your customer. Upon contract award, they meet once with your project leaders to discuss how their experience will benefit the program. They are available on call to help if/when problems arise that they probably solved before. *This* is how relevant past performance benefits your new program, and reduces performance, cost, and schedule risk.

The IPTs operate under a Charter that defines exactly what they are to accomplish, when the job is to be completed, and the resources they have under their control. This will include:

- Contract specifications, work statement, or operation,
- Delivery items and schedule,
- Resources at its disposal, and
- Budget and other constraints, etc.,

Each IPT is authorized to make all decisions defined within its Charter.

Integrated Master Plan (IMP)

The IMP is an event-based plan that provides traceability from the system level specifications through the CWBS and CSOW to the IMP, IMS, and IPTs. It is a single, contractual plan for the entire effort that describes what work will be done to accomplish all contract and CSOW activities. Just because an IMP event is conducted does not comprise completion of that task effort. All *exit criteria must be completed* before the Event can be closed. Just holding the review is not sufficient.

The IMP is normally contractual, because it describes exactly *what* you will do to accomplish the CSOW.

IPM Process

Here is how the IPM concept is organized:

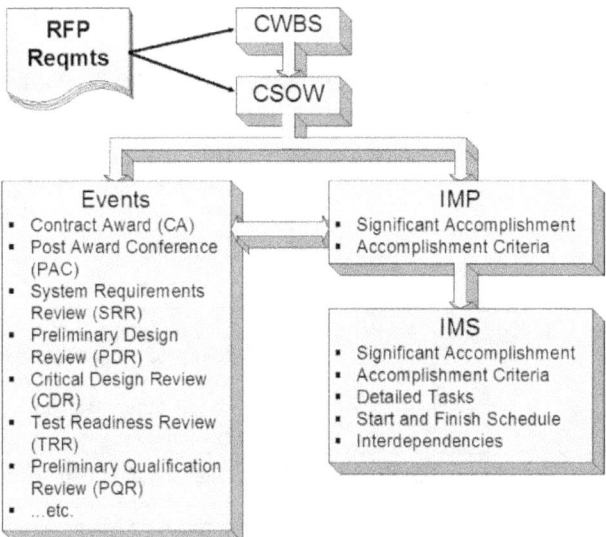

Contract Work Breakdown Structure (CWBS)

MIL-HDBK-881 is normally thought of as just a guide for invoicing your work accomplishments. It is not just for pricing—it provides an excellent structure for organizing your entire program. You can taylor it to your specific requirements.

The usual CWBS numbering scheme is very cumbersome to define and talk to, especially if you are relying on computerized numbering. A much more elegant scheme is to use an alpha-numeric scheme. Use Arabic numbers 0-9, and then Alpha numbers, A, B, C, etc., instead of going to double digits. The number of significant characters identifies the CWBS Level.

CWBS Level	Old Method	New Method
Level 1	.01	00000
Level 2	.01.01	10000
Level 3	.01.01.01	11000
Level 2	.09.01	90000
Level 2	.11.01	A0000

MIL-HDBK-881, Work Breakdown Structures (WBS), provides useful templates for various types of products (aircraft, electronics/software, missiles, ordnance, ship, space, surface vehicles) as well as the management and logistics functions required to make it happen. If your customer does not provide you with a draft WBS, use of this reference can greatly simplify your life, and it will meet Government requirements. Note that only a small part of MIL-HDBK-881 will probably be applicable to your program, so you can discard the rest.

Here is a sample for an aircraft program:

CWBS Level	CWBS Element	Title	CWBS Dictionary
1	00000	Aircraft System	This element refers to the complex of equipment (hardware/software), data, services, and facilities required to develop and produce air vehicles...
2	10000	Air Vehicle	This element refers to the complete flying aircraft. It includes airframe, propulsion, and all other installed equipment...
3	11000	Airframe	This element refers to the assembled structural and aerodynamic components of the air vehicle...

4	11100	Integration, Assembly, Test And Checkout	This element includes all efforts to provide the integration, assembly, test and checkout of all elements into the airframe...

Note the unusual CWBS numbering scheme. This is acceptable to the Government. It is a much simpler scheme than the old 1.1, 1.2, 1.3 etc., which actually becomes: 01.01, 01.02, 01.03, etc. when more than nine level elements are needed. You may add additional digits, such as 10000000 if necessary. No significant digits (i.e., 00000) denotes CWBS Level 1; one significant digit (i.e., 10000) denotes CWBS level 2; and two significant digits (i.e., 11000) denotes CWBS Level 3, and so on. This greatly simplifies numbering, and is easier to talk about. For example, CWBS Element 22000 is Program Management. If you exceed the base-ten digital limit, go into alpha-numeric numbering; 80000, 90000, A0000, B0000, etc. Now you have a base-36 numbering scheme, instead of a base-10 scheme, for which you will never have to go to double digits.

Contract Statement of Work (CSOW)

A SOW may be provided in the solicitation, either in Section C or as an attachment. Instead of a SOW, the solicitation may provide a Statement of Objectives (SOO), defining the desired results, and the contractor must define the CSOW. Be aware that after you sign the contract you will be responsible for all work specified in the RFP whether you address it or not.

RFP wording is phrased as "The Contractor shall..." to denote direction. The response is phrased as "The Contractor will..." to denote acceptance and commitment.

Contract Statement of Work (CSOW) Built From the CWBS

Here is a sample CWBS:

CWBS Level	CWBS Element	Title	CWBS Dictionary
3	22000	Program Management	This element is defined as the business and administrative planning, organizing, directing, coordinating, controlling, and approval actions designated to accomplish overall program objectives...

Re-wording the CWBS to draft the CSOW provides a direct traceability between the CWBS and the CSOW with respect to numbering, titles, and content. This greatly simplifies invoicing CSOW work to the CWBS. The CSOW will probably go into lower levels of indenture than the CWBS, and the lower levels will be summed up to the CWBS level required for invoicing.

CSOW	Title	CSOW
22000	Program Management	The Contractor shall define and implement all business and administrative planning, organizing, directing, coordinating, controlling, and approval actions needed to accomplish overall program objectives...

IMP Concept

The government defines the Milestones it must meet. These are major government program decisions defined by the DSARCs. Here is as example:

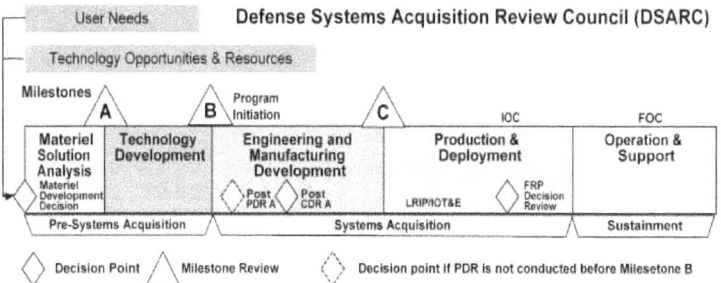

The Government Milestones are not under your control, but establish the schedule for the program Events. Your customer may identify some of the Events, but you can add additional ones. Usually you will want to schedule an Event about every three to four months in order to give your customer a "warm and fuzzy" feeling that everything is on schedule. The IMP is normally contractual because it defines what work you will do to complete the CSOW. Note that only parts of a CSOW are required for each Event, and that parts of a CSOW may be repeated for several Events because of the developing status of the CSOW.

Your IMP must include *all* contractual requirements, because it shows what you will do to complete each contractual task. It comprises three specific information requirements: the Event, Significant Accomplishments, and the Accomplishment Criteria for each accomplishment.

Events. Scheduled key contract or program decision points that establish progress towards completion of specific CSOW tasks needed for approval to continue. Note that these may be tied directly to a DSARC Milestone.

Entry Criteria. The tasks that must be completed in order to hold the Event.

Purpose. The objective and required results.

Includes. Additional considerations.

Exit Criteria. What must be accomplished in order to receive credit for the Event.

Closure. All Exit Criteria and documentation completed.

Each event will have specific criteria for accomplishment and closure. The Entry Criteria must be completed before the event can be held, and the Exit Criteria must be completed before the event can be closed. Just conducting the event is not sufficient to claim completion.

IMP Definitions

Specific Accomplishment. This is a specific action for organizational design, fabrication, or contract test activities that establish progress towards completion of a key CSOW activity, such as a desired result completed, or a discrete step in a process. Significant Accomplishments must be completions of activities that can be observed or measured by their Accomplishment Criteria. They must be unambiguous.

Accomplishment Criteria. One or more specific, observable, and measurable actions that prove you have completed a Significant Accomplishment of the IMP, and must be a *completed* work effort. "Analyzing," or "designing," words are no good, because they do not define a completed activity. "Approved," "accepted," "completed," "signed" are OK because they define a completed activity.

Narratives. These are descriptions of the company processes that you will use to manage the contract, and include such things as your Quality Assurance Program, your Safety Program, Configuration Management System, etc. Note that to be accepted as a "process," it must be documented, repeatable, and institutionalized throughout your organization, including your subcontractors and team mates.

IMP Dictionary. Note that words in your IMP have very specific meanings, and are not subject to your interpretation. The DoD IMP Dictionary is a comprehensive list, and must be followed in order to avoid misunderstanding or ambiguity. Here it is. This may be included in your response verbatim.

Term	Definition
Allocated:	The subject parameter has been subdivided or apportioned into parts and assigned to specific elements. A document that shows the allocation has been prepared and is available through the Data Accession List or other media as required for timely and complete access to the information.
Assembled:	Parts have been brought together and the pieces now form a larger element.
Assigned:	The person or asset has been committed to the designated position and is now a resource the program may utilize.
Available:	The subject item, tool, or process is in place or operational. The subject data or document has been added to the Data Accession List and is accessible through an automated information system or other media as required for timely and complete access to the information.

Term	Definition
Approved:	The subject item, data, or document has been submitted to the Government and the Government has notified the Contractor that it is acceptable.
Assessed:	The item has been evaluated by competent personnel and conclusions have been recorded.
Awarded:	The contract document has been completed and signed by both parties.
Calibrated:	The item has been functionally tested against a standard and has met the accuracy requirements of the standard.
Cleared:	Action items have been satisfactorily dispositioned
Closed:	Discrepancies have been remedied and experience/testing has validated the corrective action.
Completed:	The subject item, data, or document has been prepared and reviewed by the responsible government and contractor IPT members and has been deemed acceptable by both.
Conducted:	The planned meeting was held and results were as expected by the IPT.
Defined:	Both the contractor and the government have agreed that the subject item, data, or document has had its essential qualities and limits fixed and described in an appropriate description document which is available through the Data Accession List or other media as required for timely and complete access to the information.
Delivered:	The subject item, data, or document has been put in the hands of the intended customer.
Demonstrated :	The subject item, data, or document has been shown to be in accordance with contract requirements through performance of an un-instrumented test or a test requiring only simple quantitative measures, where success or failure is determined by observation.
Developed:	Item has been matured to the desired level.
Established:	The subject has been created and set in place in a manner consistent with its intended use (e.g. procedures, baselines established)
Evaluated:	A measured comparison of the subject with contract requirements has been completed and results are available through the Data Accession List or other media as required for timely and complete access to the information.
Fabricated:	Item has been constructed or manufactured from materials, not assembled.
Identified:	The characteristics of an item, process, or function have been made known for the first time and are shown in a document which is available through the Data Accession List or other media.
Installed:	Item has been put in place, checked out and performance verified.

Term	Definition
Integrated:	The subject has been consolidated into an entity (data, document, requirement, Configuration Item, etc.) by appropriately combining all separate requirements, functional disciplines and Configuration Item considerations.
Integrated Product Team (IPT):	The team, or portion thereof, responsible for the successful completion of the particular effort. It includes the Government member, the Contractor member, and other personnel as appropriate.
Ordered:	Formal documentation has been sent to the intended supplier.
Prepared:	The item has been created and meets its' intended purpose.
Published:	Printed and distributed, all reviews and internal approvals complete.
Received:	Document or item is in the possession of the intended recipient.
Released:	The subject data or document has received all necessary Contractor and/or Government approvals, has been completely distributed, and is available through the Data Accession List or other media as required for timely and complete access to the information.
Resolved:	Action has been taken to eliminate a problem or discrepancy and the responsible IPT agrees the action is satisfactory.
Reviewed:	The subject data or document has been examined critically and satisfies the responsible IPT members' requirements.
Scheduled:	All arrangements have been made and agreed to by all parties involved.
Signed:	A properly authorized individual has affixed a manual signature to the document.
Submitted:	Placed in the hands of the intended user or customer.
Successful	Team members (Gov't and Boeing) agree that the activity has met the intent and/or requirements of the contract.
Updated:	The subject process, data, or document has been re-evaluated using later information and adjustments have been incorporated.
Verified:	The subject item, data, or document has been proven to be in accordance with contract requirements by analysis, demonstration or tests.

Example IMP Event

Here is an example of an IMP Event definition:

Event No.	Event Name	Event Definition
2	Post Award Conference (PAC) *Scheduled for April 30, 2016*	Entry Criteria: Agreement on all contract terms, conditions, CSOW work, and procedures for contract start-up, prime contract signed

		Purpose: To initiate contract work and release contract funding. Includes: Introduction of all Government and Contractor personnel. Exit Criteria: Signed Government and Contractor contract. All teammates and subcontractors signed on and approved. Closure: Meeting documentation approved by Government and distributed.

Each Event has specific entry, activity, and exit requirements. They are specific accomplishment driven, not calendar driven. Just because the date has passed and the Event has been held, does not close the Event. The Event's Exit Criteria must be satisfied before it can be closed, and the contract work can proceed to the next phase.

IMS Concept

The contract is actually managed IAW the IMS. The IMS expands the IMP by defining the detailed task and timing of all work effort defined in the IMP. It is used as the primary tracking tool for technical and schedule status, and is based heavily upon the Accomplishment Criteria. The IMS includes all Events, accomplishments, and criteria and expected dates of each defined in the IMP, and is directly traceable to the CWBS, IMP, CSOW, IPTs, CLINs, and Data deliveries for daily program tracking. It defines Start and Finish dates and durations for all activities, and shows the interrelationships and interdependencies among related tasks, and the critical path for program completion. It may even be further expanded to individual work packages.

The IMS should be provided in Microsoft Project format, and starts with Contract Award and ends with final payment and contract closure. It is not usually contractual because any delay or changes in the work details would require a contract modification. The IMS is a "living document" and needs to be reviewed and revised as the work progresses.

Common Numbering System

RFPs that require IPM usually include a scary requirement that "...your IPM should use a common numbering system." This is for ease of tracking. If you start out with the usual CWBS and CSOW numbering system, your common numbering scheme will be very complicated and cumbersome, such as 01.01.07.3.4.1.4.1.2.1. If you use the scheme described here, it all falls together logically and easily as a combination of CWBS and CSOW numbers. Here is an example:

11100 4.1.2.1

Where:

11100 – CWBS, Level 4, AWWS System Mounting Brackets

11100 – CSOW, AWWS System Mounting Brackets. The Contractor shall provide all AWWS mounting brackets, test and evaluation, preservation, and packaging, IAW the documents listed in Section C.

4. – Test Readiness review *(Event)*

4.1 – AWWS Mounts fabrication Completed *(Significant Accomplishment)*

4.1.2 – Fabrication Complete and Quality Inspected*(Accomplishment Criteria)*

4.1.2.1 – Fabricate and Quality Check the Test Items*(Detailed Task)*

Note that this 4.4.1, 4.1.2, 4.1.2.1 IMS numbering, and renumbering as you develop your IMS and move activities around, can be done automatically by MS Project by its Outline Number function. One company that I know of numbered these activities manually, as .01.01.01.01, which is not only extremely difficult and time consuming, but, well, stupid. Any change early in the schedule requires manually changing several hundred entries.

Example IMS

Here is a tabular example of an IMS in MS Project that could be provided in your text write-up, which shows the Event for the Post Award Conference (PAC) and Interim Project Review (IPR).

CWBS	CSOW	Event No.	Events, Accomplish., Criteria, Tasks	Dur.	Start	Finish
91000	91000	2	**.PAC & IPR**	20d	3/13	5/10
91000	91000	2.1	Entry Criteria Completed	1d	3/28	4/28
91000	91000	2.2	PM & SE Processes & Resources Available	12d	3/13	4/28
91000	91000	2.2.1	SE Processes Available	12d	3/13	4/28
20000	20000	2.2.1.1	Prepare SEMP	12d	3/13	4/28
31000	31000	2.2.1.2	Prepare & Approve ITP	12d	3/13	4/28

20000	20000	2.2.1.3	Implement System Design Notebook Documentatio n	11d	3/14	4/28
20000	20000	2.2.1.4	Develop, Document, and Implement CAIV	11d	3/14	4/28
20000	20000	2.2.1.5	Establish SWG	11d	3/14	4/28
24000	24000	2.2.1.6	Develop, Implement, and Maintain QC Program	11d	3/14	4/28
20000	20000	2.3.1	Conduct PAC	1d	3/15	4/29
20000	20000	2.3.2	Conduct IPR	1d	3/16	4/30
20000	20000	2.4	Exit Criteria and Closure completed	0d	3/16	4/30

As you develop your IMS, you will probably revise the Significant Accomplishments and Accomplishment Criteria that comprise your IMP. Not to worry: After you have finished your IMS you can "pluck" your revised IMP from the IMS by a simple Microsoft Project filter. Your actual IMS will include task interrelationships, and the Gantt Chart bar graphs. You will probably also need to show a Critical Path. In Project you can add the responsible IPTs, CLIN references, CDRL deliveries, and resources, such as individual people, and adjust their number and work schedules in order to meet the delivery schedule.

PART IX – RESPONSE REVIEWS AND THE END GAME

How to benefit from your last chance to "get it right"

Pink Team Review

A Pink Team Review should be held as soon as you have organized your response, and mapped all of the solicitation requirements to one or more response sections or paragraphs. This early review will verify that you are on the right track, and should eliminate any major structural response changes during the final Red Team Review when time is short. Your Pink Team should comprise the same people as your Red Team. The Pink Team should review your response organization against the solicitation requirements. This should be in outline format only, with no written draft. This is to avoid confusing your final Red Team with memories of information that might no longer be included. The results of your Pink Team should ensure that your response outline complies with RFP Section L, and that all solicitation program and response requirements have been identified and mapped to the correct response sections and paragraphs. Ideally your response themes and win strategies should be assigned where they will be most effective.

Red Team Reviews

Generally, scheduling your Red Team Review about one week or a week and a half to two weeks before submission is appropriate. Members should be outside people who are not familiar with your company or your response, other than during their Pink Team Review. They should be familiar with the specific evaluation factor disciplines, and if they are familiar with your customer and his/her interests in this solicitation so much the better. The Red Team should see only what the Government evaluators will see. Refrain from any detailed explanation of your program or offering that might skew their impressions—you won't be there to brief the Government evaluators.

Timing of your reviews is always difficult, and a "best guess" at best. About 1 to 2 weeks before submission is a good compromise. Schedule too early, and many corrections will be needed, resulting in either a repeat Red Team Review, or much of the submitted response will not have been reviewed by the Red Team. Schedule too late, and even though the response will be more mature and fewer changes required, there is not much time left. Response quality may actually deteriorate if you have too much time, because inventors, authors, and management will use the extra time to try to make the response "even more better," and lose the succinct character of the presentation. The following figure illustrates the problem:

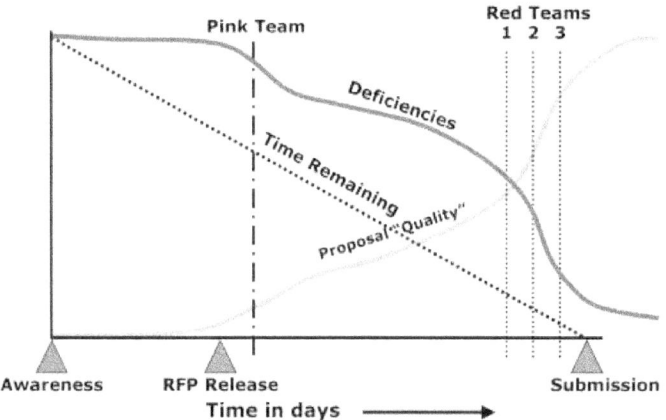

Red Team Review Plan

A structured Red Team Review is critical. The objective is to provide an impartial, outside assessment of your response, against the solicitation requirements, as a "devil's advocate." Your Red Team should be identified, approved, and committed immediately after receipt of the formal solicitation. You should identify specific outside experts for each discipline because they will not be influenced by what they know of your company capabilities outside of your response. They must base their evaluation only on the material presented in your response. Company personnel may be included, but their judgment will be biased and unreliable. Your plan should establish the review process and schedule, and your Red Team members must commit to the schedule. Your Red Team may or may not review the Cost Volume.

> **War Story:**
> *For one Fortune 500 Company, the Technical Panel was composed of the company's Vice President of engineering and his staff. I had set up a review process that required scoring the response against what I estimated to be the Evaluation Standards. In the debriefing to the response team and the company General Manager, the Vice President of Engineering reported: "We reviewed the response and both I and my staff thought it was the best proposal we have ever written. It had all of our win themes and information. It was great. Then my staff asked if they could go back to their real jobs. I told them no, that we had to review and score the response against the evaluation criteria in accordance with the Red Team Review Plan. And guess what? We found that our response was virtually non-responsive! It would have been a certain loser!"*

Sample Red Team Review Plans and score sheets are provided in *Appendix A, Red Team Review Plan(s).*

Sanity Checklist for Red Team Draft and Production

The following check list will be helpful to your reviewers:

Check List	Yes	No
Does the entire response comply with the solicitation Section L – Instructions to offerors, and also follow the RFP Section M – Evaluation Factors for Award?		
Is the story presented in the text logical and understandable?		
Does the story stay "on track" with no superfluous wording?		
Are your win strategies and win themes apparent, are they credible, and are they located in the best places?		
Will a reader just skimming the sections get your main message in 30 seconds?		
Did an expert on a section make a final check to ensure technical accuracy?		
Make "8 Cs check:		
• Clarity		
• Completeness		
• Conciseness		
• Consistency		
• Content		
• Continuity		
• Correctness		
• Credibility		

Red Team Review Process

For the actual Red Team Review, your General Manager should welcome the Red Team, tell it where the bathrooms and refreshments are, and announce that lunch will be brought in. Your Program Manager or Capture Manager should brief it on the program *from the customer's point of view, not yours*; and your Response Manager should brief it on how it should review and mark up the materials and fill out the score sheets. Follow these general guidelines to help ensure a successful Red Team Review.

- Appoint a Red Team Leader.
- Red Team Leader identifies review panels and panel leaders.
- Everyone reads the Cover Letter and Executive Summary.
- Each response section is reviewed by more than one person.
- No reviewer has to review the whole thing.
- Authors and book bosses should attend the opening and be introduced, then only be available if needed.
- Reviewers should each have a copy of the RFP Sections L, M, and Specifications, the Executive Summary, and copies of their review material
- Complete copies of the RFP should be available
- Remove all black pens, and allow only red pens for marking up the draft.

- Document major deficiencies on Response Deficiency Reports

Reviewers may mark up the draft itself, but add their initials to each page for future reference in case of questions or clarification. If reviewers use black pens, their remarks may be missed—they should use red pens.

Be specific in your comments, and avoid nit picking and grammatical comments. Offer constructive suggestions for corrections. Comment on what is good and should not be changed, as well as what needs correcting. Criticize the work, not the author. Be specific: writing "This part stinks!" will not be helpful.

Hold a plenary session at the end of the first day to determine how is it going, whether the response is good enough to review, whether this review process is working and if not, then how you should proceed.

The plenary session sometimes alerts you that the response is too rough for a productive review, in which case you must change the review process in order to benefit from the Red Team's perspective.

War Story:

On one proposal, written by a Type X autocratic company, we had what one consultant called The Red Army *for a Red Team. It was huge. At the first day's end plenary session, it was apparent that the proposal was so rough and disjointed that it was impossible to review. That night I planned my course of action, and the next morning I listed all of the proposal sections on the white board and announced: "You are no longer a Red Review Team, you are now a Tiger Team! If you know enough to evaluate this proposal you know enough to fix it!" I then assigned each section to an individual and told them to fix it! This was the only way we got the proposal out on time. But it still was a loser because it had fatal technical flaws that I was powerless to correct.*

An example of an effective Red Team Review is described in *Appendix B, A Red Team Blue Print, A Case Study.*

Red Team Review Debriefing

After the response is reviewed the reviewers should hand in their comments and Response Deficiency Reports to their panel leaders, who consolidate them and resolve any problems. After the reviews are completed, the Red Team Leader prepares a summary presentation of the results. This presentation should be only top-level comments—details should be provided in the individual reports. The entire response team should be present, and only clarification questions are permitted. No detailed explanations should be allowed from the authors. If authors want specific help in correcting their material they should work with the reviewers after the formal review. Critique the program and the response, do not criticize the authors.

Recovering From Red Team Reviews

Red Team Reviews are always disruptive and can be demoralizing, but you must recover and finalize your response. You must complete final editing and formatting, obtain final approval from your top management, publish your submission according to the solicitation requirements, quality check your submission materials, package them for delivery, and deliver them IAW the solicitation instructions *to the letter*!

The Red Team makes recommendations, not decisions. Your program and response managers make decisions. Hand out the draft mark ups to the respective authors with instructions: "Make the changes, and if you have questions, see me."

Decide how to respond to the Response Deficiency Reports. Don't make unnecessary changes just to make it "even more better."

The Model Contract

Completed sections, such as the Model Contract, can be prepared and printed at any time. The Model Contract (sometimes called other names) is your "Signed Contract" obligation. It includes the RFP:

- Section A – DD Form 33 and all SF 30s
- Part I – The Schedule
- Part II – Contract Clauses
- Part III – List of Attachments
- Part IV – Representations And Instructions
  - o   Section K, Representations, Certifications, and other Statements of Offeror (Fill in the blanks and sign where indicated)
  - o   Section L, Instructions, Conditions, and Notices to Offerors
  - o   Section M, Evaluation Factors for Award

Gold Team Review

Final approval must be made by your company top management for program and response submission, including pricing. They must refrain from any last minute "improvements to make it even more better." After the final corrections, editing, and formatting have been completed, don't mess with it! This can (and has) really screw(ed) up your submission copy. There are no minor, last minute changes. Let me repeat that: *There are no minor last minute changes*!

War Story:

After the final draft was sent to the commercial printers, about 90 miles away, the proposal manager came to me for a small correction to the 25-page Executive Summary that I had prepared. She only needed to add an extra bullet to an existing bullet list. She said she would telephone the printer, with whom she had worked many times before and he could add the extra bullet. I objected, but she insisted, and said there was no problem, it was such a simple addition. I finally agreed, and thought that I should go to double check the addition. But I was tired—I had been working 12-14 hours a day straight for four weeks. I let my guard down. That Sunday we got the printed proposal. I double checked the Executive Summary to be sure everything was OK. It was not OK! The added bullet had slipped down below the title of the following paragraph. Now it made

---

no sense, and indicated sloppy work. Not a good impression! Sunday afternoon we had to telephone the printer, who had to call in his staff, correct and reprint the entire, 25-page, saddle-stitched, full color Executive Summary, and drive it down to us. As a result, we had to use our backup plan in order to deliver the proposal on time on Tuesday.

Ideally top management will have been involved in program definition, response organization, and preparation so there are no surprises or significant changes needed.

Also, do not arbitrarily reduce your price at this point because it will be inconsistent with the work promised in your CSOW. The Government may conduct a "should cost" assessment to determine what your CSOW work would cost based upon your audited DCAA cost numbers. Your price will be assessed upon this "should cost" estimate, not your quoted price. Be sure that your cost response is consistent with your Contract Statement of Work.

Printing and Packing

Follow the RFP Section L printing and packing instructions exactly. Prepare a Response Format Specification and Publication Plan to define exactly how many copies of each hard copy and/or electronic (CD) is printed, as well as how to handle any classified sections. Normally print two sets. The second set is the backup submission if your primary delivery fails. If not needed, it becomes your internal copies. Be sure that backup production equipment is sanding by for emergencies. Ensure that your packing and delivery comply with RFP delivery instructions.

At this point, everyone is burned out, and the final printing and packaging must be a "no brainer." Put a check sheet on each and every binder for checking off every requirement (i.e., cover, spine, title page, TOC, List of Illustrations, text, illustrations, tabbed dividers, etc.). You will be amazed at how many times you will find a Table of Contents, List of Illustrations, or divider pages missing. You should pack and label the cost volume(s) and CDs separately from the other volumes.

Response Delivery

Prepare and publish a Delivery Plan. Be sure to review it just before delivery in case delivery instructions have been changed by an RFP amendment. Determine:

- How the response will be delivered.
- How the backup response will be delivered.
- Who the courier is for each response set.
- Who is responsible for making the flight/driving arrangements.
- Who will the courier contact in case of a problem, or to report that the response has been delivered.
- Stress the importance of arriving at the delivery location early.
- Be sure to get a receipt.

> **War Story:**
> On one proposal, the Vice President of Marketing was told, by the program manager: "Don't deliver the proposal too early!" There is absolutely no reason for this instruction—only the Government Contracting officer is authorized to accept competitive proposals and it's too late for any competitor to benefit from knowing that or what you submitted. The Vice President was chatting with a friend when he realized that he had only 15 minutes to deliver the proposal. The next thing he realized was that he was in the wrong building! By the time he got to the right building, he was 5 minutes late. Too late! The proposal was refused! That was probably the toughest phone call he ever made in his entire life! There were two courses of action: One, he could be fired for failing to deliver the proposal; or Two, the president would be absolutely certain that this man would never miss a deadline again! Fortunately for the vice President, the later choice saved his job.

Response Delivery

This function is the only one for which the deadline cannot be ignored. Hand deliver your response at the time and to the place specified in the solicitation. You have spent a lot of money, time, and effort—don't try to save on air fare now and risk a note from FedEx: "Gee! We're sorry, but our truck broke down." If FedEx, UPS, or other carriers fail to deliver on time, the best you can hope for is a refund of your postage—small consolation for hundreds of thousands of dollars—maybe even millions—wasted. Also, allow for weather or flight cancellations. The only responses that can be trusted to mailing are responses to the United States Postal System—you can Express Mail them for next day delivery, and if they are late, the USPS will not complain! (Or so I've heard.)

- **Hand deliver**
  - ## Hand Deliver
    - # HAND DELIVER!!!

Take the Rest of the Day Off

Now that your response is finished and submitted, you can take a well deserved rest and await any questions to be answered before you sign the contract and plan the victory party.

PART X – POST SUBMISSION ACTIONS
What to do after you submit your response

Post Delivery Questions and Responses

If you are judged "in the competitive range" you will be given a chance to correct any deficiencies and to clarify any confusing material in your response. This is required by the FARs and DFARs. How do you qualify to be in the competitive range? This is decided by the Contracting Officer. The usual criterion is whether your response has sufficient merit to convince the Contracting Officer to give you another chance. Practically speaking, however, it is also a matter of how many responses are submitted. If there are only two submissions you can be sure to be in the competitive range or there is no "horse race" for price negotiations. If there are many submissions the criterion will be much more strict.

There are basically three types of Evaluation Notices (ENs) that you would receive:

Clarification Requests (CRs). These are questions that enable you to clarify some point(s) in your response that were unclear or not sufficiently justified. These points might have been scored yellow or even green, but the Contracting Officer needs more information to justify your response to the Source Selection Authority.

Deficiency Reports (DRs). These are questions for response topics that failed to meet one or more of the minimum standards. These were probably scored yellow or maybe even red. Your chances of given this opportunity improve as the number of responses decreases.

Best and Final Offering (BaFO). Although the FARs and DFARs proscribe against the government using Best and Final demands in order to lower your price, it happens. Be careful of reducing your price too much, however, because the Government will become suspicious and you will still lose. And remember that any price reductions you promise must still pay for all of the CSOW tasks you have promised.

Mostly these ENs are self explanatory, and should be addressed with equal vigor as your response itself. The instructions will provide you with detailed requirements for your response, including format, page limitations, and submission deadline. Usually you are forbidden to include any new or additional information—you are to correct or clarify only the material in your original submission.

Lessons Learned and Customer Follow-up

Conducting a "Lessons Learned" exercise after each response is a good idea, but be aware that from a self-assessment you can only assess how well your "process" worked, not the actual quality of your response. The best assessment you can have is a candid discussion with your customer. You can expect a completely honest report if you win, but if you have lost, your customer may be reluctant to be candid in fear of a protest.

Protests

The solicitation will include information about contacting an ombudsman to protest if you believe that you have been treated unfairly. But be careful about protesting—you don't want to get a reputation for causing trouble. But if you really have a gripe, don't hesitate to present all of your documentation and protest the decision of the SSA.

Obtaining Customer Feedback

If you send the individuals responsible for the loss to find out why they screwed up, imagine them coming back and telling the company president, "Boy! I sure screwed up on that one!" I think not. What generally happens is they tell their boss: "They really liked our response! Said we had done a lot of good work and had some really good ideas."

A knowledgeable but "disinterested" individual—let's call him or her the Responses Quality Assurance Manager (PQAM)—should establish a cordial, trusting rapport with all of your potential customers, with whom both parties are at ease with candid questions, critiques, and observations, long before RFPs are released or responses submitted. It may be from your Quality Assurance, Business Development, Contracts, or Response Administration organizations. It might even be a retired Chief Executive, President, Vice President of Engineering, or a consultant. During these candid conversations with your customer, it's a good idea to send only one person in order to preclude the possibilities for confrontation, argument, or any other negative reaction. The purpose is to understand and the attitude is humility.

Lessons Learned on HOE Response—A Case Study

These Lessons Learned from GiantCorp's *Homing Overlay Experiment* response was developed from the formal letter from the Government Contracting officer. You may have noticed that these conditions are covered in many of the preceding lectures.

- Poor illustrations
- Confusing format
- Much too wordy
- No two-part captions
- Separated art and text
- Poor grammar
- Misspelled words and typos
- Inconsistent units and references

Now You Know How To:

Respond to New Business Opportunities of the Federal Government with new skills for a job that nobody really wants to do.

May the Force be with you.

Appendix A

Red Team Review
Plan(s)

Red Team Review Plan

Proposal for

ADVANCED WIDGET WARNING SYSTEM
FULL SCALE DEVELOPMENT

RFP PTC-90-R-1234

Review: 14-16 Mar 2016
Debriefing: 16 Mar 2016
Time: 1500 hrs.
Place: **DOD CONTRACTOR, INC.**
        Building #2
        Main Conference Room
Red Team Leader: Charlie Buck

RED TEAM REVIEW AGENDA

Monday, 14 Mar 2016
DCI, Bldg. #2, Main Conference. Room

0800	Welcome	Company President
0810	Program Background	- Donald Plummer, Pgm. Mgr.
0830	Red Team Review Instructions	- Charlie Buck, Red Tm. Ldr.
0900	Individual Review of Volumes	- Panel Members
1200	- - - - - - - - - - - - - - - - - - L U N C H - - - ---- -- - - - - - - - - - - - -
1300	Individual Review of Volumes	- Panel Members
1600	Plenary Meeting	- Panel Members
1800	- - - - - - - - - - - --- - -- D I N N E R - - - - - - --- - - - - - - - - -
1900	Individual Review of Volumes-	Panel Members

Tuesday, 15 Mar 2016
DCI, Bldg. #2, Main Conference. Room

0800	Individual Review of Volumes	- Panel Members
1200	- - - - - - - - - - - - - - - - - - L U N C H - - - ---- -- - - - - - - - - - - - -
1300	Individual Review of Volumes	- Panel Members
1600	Panel Meeting (Plenary)	- Panel Members

> Panel Members start "one-on-one" discussions with volume/section managers as appropriate.

1800- - - - - - - - - - - - - --- - - - - - - -- D I N N E R -
1900	Prepare for Volume Debrief	- Panel/Chairman

Wednesday, 16 Mar 2016
DCI, Bldg. #2, Main Conference. Room

0800	Red Team Debrief of Volumes-	Panel Chairman/members Vol. Mgrs, Authors
1200	- - - - - - - - - - - - - - - - - L U N C H - - - ---- -- - - - - - - - - - - - -
1300	Chair Debriefs (Plenary)	Panel/Chairman
1500	Exec. Summary Review (Plenary)	Panel/Chairman
1600	Continue as Required/Adjourn	

OBJECTIVE

The objective of a Red Team Review is to have a knowledgeable but unbiased team review the proposal AGAINST THE RFP through the eyes of the (Government) evaluators as a devil's advocate.

On 9-14 January, 2016, the Red Team reviewed our win strategies (Pink Team Review), which were then distributed so that all proposal managers and authors would understand our approach, and could tell the same story in their proposal sections. By formulating effective strategies and agreeing upon them, we could tell a unified story. The Pink Team also reviewed our proposed assignments of RFP requirements to the Bookplan paragraphs (i.e., RFP Section L requirements). This confirmed the basic proposal structure, and was intended to eliminate the need for major changes later at this formal Red Team Review.

EXPECTED EVALUATION METHOD

The RFP specifies that the PROPOSALS TRAINING COMMAND Source Selection Evaluation Board will evaluate the proposals in the following three areas, which we expect to be weighted approximately as follows:

Area 1.0	TECHNICAL	50% of total score
Area 2.0	UNIT/LIFE CYCLE COST	30% of total score
Area 3.0	MANAGEMENT	20% of total score

Although the RFP identifies COST as less important than TECHNICAL, remember that ACQUISITION PRICE is ALWAYS NUMBER ONE!! Furthermore, this RFP (Section M, Paragraph A.) warns: "...the offeror's price will be a substantial factor in the Source Selection Authority's (SSA's) decision."

PROPOSAL ORGANIZATION/PREPARATION APPROACH

Using the RFP Section M, Evaluation Factors for Award, an estimate was made of which RFP specific evaluation subfactors will be used to evaluate each RFP requirement, and a selection made of the RFP evaluation Subfactorss that should provide the most advantage to us for each of our win strategies.

One output of this process is a strawman Source Selection Evaluation Plan (SSEP) that lists all RFP requirements and win strategies against the estimated RFP evaluation sub-elements, similar to the expected PROPOSALS TRAINING COMMAND Source Selection Plan. Another output is a set of Storyboard Requirements that, for each RFP Section L paragraph requirement, identify the specific RFP Section M evaluation factor under which it will probably be evaluated, and lists all RFP requirements and win strategies to be addressed (or at least considered) in that paragraph. This is essentially a "cut-and-paste" of the RFP requirements to the RFP Section L. Sets of these Storyboard Requirements are provided for your convenience in assessing our responsiveness to the RFP.

RED TEAM EVALUATION PROCEDURE

1. Please familiarize yourself with this evaluation plan and with the RFP requirements provided in this Evaluator Workbook. Complete RFPs are available if you need them, but this workbook includes the RFP sections you will probably need.

2. Red Team Panel Leaders will be assigned for each RFP evaluation area (i.e., Technical, Unit/Life Cycle Cost, and Management).

3. Skim through the proposal draft for an overview of our proposed offering.

4. Score the proposal using the "Scoring Method" scale AGAINST YOUR INTERPRETATION OF THE RFP REQUIREMENTS (The RFP requirements listed in the Storyboard Requirements printouts will be most convenient for you). You do not have to read the proposal in its entirety; look only for the information you need in order to score the evaluation subfactors, because this is the way the customer will evaluate the proposal. You will be evaluating only the Operational Capability and Management Volumes, and the Executive Summary. To evaluate the Cost areas, review the technical and management stories with a view to their convincing the evaluators that our approach is the lowest, credible acquisition price—that any lower price would incur unacceptable cost, schedule and performance risk. This numerical scoring discipline may seem a bother, but no other method has proven to uncover proposal or program weaknesses as effectively.

5. In addition to scoring each factor, please complete a Proposal Deficiency Report for each comment you have which requires resolution, and specify a Priority:
    MUST FIX: Fatal defect; high probability of being scored "Non-responsive," "Unacceptable," or "Marginal."
    SHOULD FIX: Would probably weaken our competitive position, but would probably still be judged "Acceptable."
    MAY FIX: Minor irritant; if time does not permit changes, it probably would not reduce our score.

6. You may also mark the draft copy directly, but if you do so, please use a red marker and mark the page with a paper clip or staple so that we don't overlook your comments.

    ## SCORING METHOD

    Use the following 5-point scoring:

    5 – OUTSTANDING (Blue). Response meets requirements and indicates an exceptional approach and understanding of the requirements that exceed the RFP requirements, and that excess had substantial benefits to the Government. Strengths far outweigh any weaknesses. Risk of unsuccessful performance is very low.

    4 – GOOD (Purple). Response meets requirements and indicates a thorough approach and understanding of the requirements.

Response contains strengths which outweigh any weaknesses. Risk of unsuccessful performance is low.

3 – ACCEPTABLE (Green). Response meets requirements and indicates an adequate approach and understanding of the requirements. Strengths and weaknesses are offsetting or will have little or no impact on contract performance. Risk of unsuccessful performance is no worse than moderate. May fix

2 – MARGINAL (Yellow). Response does not clearly meet requirements and has not demonstrated an adequate approach and understanding of the requirements. The response has one or more weaknesses which are not offset by strengths. Risk of unsuccessful performance is high. Should fix.

0 - NON-RESPONSIVE/UNACCEPTABLE (Red). Proposal does not meet requirements and contains one or more deficiencies. Proposal is un-awardable. A fatal defect. Must fix.

You may use intermediate scores, such as 3.5, if you wish. Write your scores in the appropriate boxes of the EVALUATION MATRICES. Note that the evaluation is against both the Specific Criteria and the General Criteria as specified in solicitation Section M, Evaluation Factors for Award.

ASSESSMENT OF RISK

Risk has become very important to Government program managers. During your discussions, be alert to risk implications, and consider them in the strategies. The following excerpt from AFR 70-15, Source Selection Policy and Procedures, is offered for your guidance:

"a. Identification and assessment of the risks associated with each proposal is essential. The following definitions of risk should be used:

"**(1) HIGH (H)** -- Likely to cause significant serious disruption of schedule, increase in cost, or degradation of performance even with special contractor emphasis and close government monitoring.

"**(2) MODERATE (M)** -- Can potentially cause some disruption of schedule, increase in cost, or degradation of performance. However, special contractor emphasis and close government monitoring will probably be able to overcome difficulties.

"**(3) LOW (L)** -- Has little potential to cause disruption of schedule, increase in cost, or degradation of performance. Normal contractor effort and normal government monitoring will probably be able to overcome difficulties."

This regulation requires the acquisition activity or program office to furnish the Source Selection Evaluation Board an independent assessment of anticipated risks, and requires that offerors include a risk analysis in their proposals. The proposal evaluators must consider all of this and make an independent judgment of the probability of success, the impact of failure, and the alternatives available to meet the requirements.

Note that a proposed "low risk" approach suggests "business as usual," and that any "moderate" or "high" risk approach should include provisions for "special contractor emphasis and close government monitoring" to overcome the difficulties.

RED TEAM DEBRIEFING

The Red Team Leader should determine the type and format of debriefing appropriate for this review. The Red Team Leader will consolidate your individual numerical scores and present them at a formal debriefing. Each Red Team Member will present a summary of his/her comments. The Red Team Leader will collect and consolidate the comments and deliver the package to the Proposal Manager to copy, distribute, and file.

Your comments will be valuable in structuring our proposal and will certainly increase our win probability. Thank you for your help.

Glenn Edwards
Proposal Manager

RED TEAM REVIEW SCORE SHEETS

The evaluators will score your proposal against their Source Selection Plan (SSP), not against other proposals, and not even against the solicitation Section M, Evaluation Factors for Award. The SSP defines the "Standards" against which each proposal will be scored.

The evaluators score how well your proposal satisfies the standards for each specific evaluation factor or subfactor by applying the assessment criteria defined in the RFP Section M, Evaluation Factors for Award. These assessment criteria usually comprise understanding the requirements, compliance with requirements, soundness of approach, past performance, risk, and sometimes other general criteria. The standards are the minimum acceptable criteria for the "acceptable range." The evaluators will use a score sheet similar to the one shown below.

Fill out this form, add as many pages as you need, and prepare one set of pages for each volume that your Red Team will be scoring. Insert the specific evaluation factors or subfactors in the headers, and revise the left hand column to show the assessment criteria for your specific RFP. Direct your Red Team to score your proposal IAW this plan.

RED TEAM REVIEW SCORE SHEETS

Volume: _____ **Evaluator:** _____

Specific Evaluation Factor/Subfactor:	Factor or Subfactor	Factor or Subfactor	Factor or Subfactor	Factor or Subfactor
Assessment Criteria:				
Understanding the Requirements				
Soundness of Approach				
Compliance with Requirements				
Past Performance				
Risk				
TOTAL				

Response Name	Control Number:
Proposal Deficiency Report	Score:
Date: _____	Priority:

Proposal Volume:	Red Team Review Panel:
Proposal Paragraph:	Red Team Reviewer:
	Author:

Assessment Criteria:	Understanding the Requirements	Soundness of Approach	Compliance With Requirements	Past Performance	Risk Assessment and Mitigation	Other
Score:						

APPLICABLE EVALUATION CRITERIA or WIN STRATEGY: *(Reference the RFP or Win Strategy.)*

NATURE of DEFICIENCY: *(What is the problem with the story? Be concise.)*

SUMMARY of EFFECTS of DEFICIENCY: *(How would deficiency affect the program if not corrected?)*

SPECIFIC RECOMMENDATIONS: *(Suggest specific changes or wording to correct the deficiency.)*

ACTION:	ACTION COMPLETED and APPROVED BY:

Alternate Red Team Review Scoring Method

Red Team Review Score Sheets _____Factor

Red Team Reviewer: _____

Score each subfactor: **Yes,   No,   Maybe.**

For each factor/subfactor scored "No" please fill out a Proposal Deficiency Report, with suggestions for correcting the problem.

FACTOR 1: _____

(Enter the solicitation Section M – Evaluation Factors for Award for this factor.)

SUBFACTOR 1: _____

Does this section show that the response meets or exceeds the Section M requirement to (enter the detailed information for this subfactor from the Section M).

Understanding of the Problem	Compliance with Requirements.	Soundness of approach
__Yes __No __Maybe	__Yes __No ___Maybe	__Yes __No ___Maybe

Comment/Improvement suggestions:

SUBFACTOR 2: _____

Does this section show that the response meets or exceeds the Section M requirement to (enter the detailed information for this subfactor from the Section M).

Understanding of the Problem	Compliance with Requirements.	Soundness of approach
__Yes __No __Maybe	__Yes __No ___Maybe	__Yes __No ___Maybe

Comment/Improvement suggestions:

SUBFACTOR 1: _____

Does this section show that the response meets or exceeds the Section M requirement to (enter the detailed information for this subfactor from the Section M).

Understanding of the Problem	Compliance with Requirements.	Soundness of approach
__Yes __No __Maybe	__Yes __No ___Maybe	__Yes __No ___Maybe

Comment/Improvement suggestions:

Appendix B

A Red Team
Blue Print

A Case Study

A Red Team Blue Print, A Case Study

"This Red Team was like night and day [compared to our last one]—it was the best organized that I've ever seen. We had everything that we needed. It was actually enjoyable!"   *V.P. and General Manager*

What do your Red Team Reviewers need in order to give you the "most bang" for your dollar? Do you simply put them in a big room, give them a quick briefing on your understanding of the program, a few instructions including where to find coffee and the bathrooms, hand them a three hundred-page RFP and a two hundred-page proposal, and ask them to see if you missed anything?

A good, worthwhile (meaning: "worth the huge interruption and distraction") Red Team doesn't just "happen" by itself—it takes a lot of advance preparation effort, organization, and set up. Here's how we planned and executed the Red Team Review that resulted in the accolades noted at the lead in to this article.

A Pink Team blueprint—First, we had a "Pink Team," immediately after we had mapped the RFP requirements to our proposal outline, This Pink Team comprised the same individuals who would later review our proposal draft. The objective of the Pink Team was to confirm that we were answering all of the RFP questions and including our win themes and strategies in our proposal where the evaluators expect to find them. This sanity check, before we started actual writing, would avoid major re-organizing at the last minute. With this confirmation (and redirection, if needed) we knew that our proposal was on the right track, and that post Red Team changes would consist of rewriting, not major reorganizing!

The best individuals for the Red Team are people who don't know a lot about your company—the only thing they should know about your company is what they read in your proposal, because that more accurately replicates your customer's evaluation environment. Given that "ideal," for economy most Red Teams comprise senior management or specialists from your company or other divisions, perhaps supplemented by one or two consultants. When this happens, it is all the more important to follow a structured review that evaluates your proposal against the RFP Section M, Evaluation Factors for Award, and actually scores it against the evaluation criteria. The scoring can be numerical (1, 2, 3, etc), subjective (+, OK, -), or color-coded (Red – Unacceptable/Non-responsive; Yellow – Marginal; Green – Acceptable; Purple – Good, or Blue – Outstanding with added benefits to the customer). We prefer the color coding because it does not try to "measure a brick with a micrometer," because it is very graphic, and because it is the scheme that the DoD evaluators will probably use. The value of actually scoring the proposal is that it forces the reviewers' attention on the evaluation criteria and results in a more objective review.

The importance of a structured review—On one proposal, where the Technical Panel Leader was the company's Vice President of Engineering, and his panel was his staff, his debriefing to the proposal team underscored the value of a structured review: "We read the proposal. It is one of the best proposals we have ever done! We looked great! The proposal included all of our themes and win strategies! It was a sure winner! My staff asked that, since we were done, could they go back to their 'real jobs.' I told them 'no,' that we still had to 'score' the proposal against the RFP Section M. Guess what? Even though our proposal read great, it was *virtually non-responsive!* It was a *certain loser!*"

How DoD doesn't evaluate proposals—Before we set up the formal Red Team Review process, a few words are in order to explain exactly how DoD customers do and don't evaluate proposals. First, let's clear up some popular misconceptions. The evaluators:

- *Do not* read the entire proposal straight through.
- *Do not* score proposals against each other.
- *Do not* score proposals against the RFP— even against Section M.
- *Do not* score the Specific Evaluation Factors.

How DoD does evaluate proposals—Here is how the Federal Acquisition Regulations require them to evaluate and score competitive proposals, and these regulations are generally followed very closely in order to avoid protests.

The evaluation organization is organized into a Source Selection Evaluation Board (SSEB) (or team) that will evaluate and score the proposals. There is also a Source Selection Advisory Council (SSAC) that will advise the decision maker about other factors germane to the source acquisition (i.e., political, budgetary, programmatic, etc.). Finally, there is the Source Selection Authority (SSA) who is the specific individual who will make the actual decision, based upon all of the information available.

This SSA is under incredible pressure from the eventual users, competing interests, Government oversight agencies, Congress, the White House (on large programs), and the public. It is a safe assumption that the SSA makes the decision that is safest for his or her career, and that can be fully justified to the losing bidders' congress-people.

A fully justified, winning approach—For example, in 1991, then Secretary of Defense Dick Cheney justified, to Senator C.S. Bond, his selection of the F/A-18E/F over the F-14:

> "In selecting the F/A-18E/F, we considered not only performance and unit price, but also a host of other factors which impact on cost, such as weapon system reliability, maintainability, safety, maintenance costs, squadron manning requirements and cost per flight hour.

> "In the final analysis the F/A-18E/F was the clear choice over the F-14. It is three times more reliable, twice as easy to maintain, has a safety record which is fifty percent better, requires about twenty-five percent fewer maintenance personnel, and costs about twenty-five

percent less to operate per flight hour. When combined, these factors clearly show that the F/A-18E/F is the more cost effective aircraft."

It's hard to argue against that, and your Red Team should ensure that your proposal is equally convincing. To do so, it has to convey a powerful message to the evaluators.

How the SSEB scores proposals—The SSEB will usually be divided into Panels that represent the disciplines described in the RFP Section M, Specific Evaluation Factors. These specific factors are not scored directly, but indicate the various disciplines of interest to the SSEB. There will likely be a Technical Panel, a Management Panel, and a Cost Panel (costs are not scored, but they are evaluated, usually for realism and reasonableness). The Technical Panel may be further divided into Sub-Panels for specific disciplines such as (for an aircraft) Performance, Airframe, Propulsion, Flight Controls, Weapons, computer systems, etc.

Now it gets a little tricky: The SSEB scores the proposals in accordance with the approved and published Source Selection Plan (SSP), not against the RFP Section M. We've seen only one RFP with this SSP information included. The SSP is not the RFP Section M, but Section M is based upon the SSP. The SSP must be approved and locked in the safe before any proposals are accepted in order to preclude any biases put into the SSP to favor a competitor. The SSP cannot differ significantly from the RFP Section M, but it expands Section M to provide specific guidance to the evaluators by identifying the "standards" against which the proposals will be evaluated.

For each specific evaluation factor or subfactor, the SSP will define that factor or subfactor (this usually follows the RFP Section M Specific Evaluation Factor/Subfactor fairly closely), and then states: "The standards are met when the offeror:" then follows a list of very specific quantitative or qualitative values that comprise the minimum acceptable requirements for the proposal to be in the "acceptable range." These will relate to the minimum specification and SOW requirements that the customer will accept.

Now, here's the tricky part: The SSEB does not score the specific factors *per se*, but scores each standard according to the RFP Section M Assessment Criteria: Understanding the problem, Compliance with requirements, and Soundness of approach. The SSEB will give each of these assessment factors a score (either numerical or color-coded) for each standard.

Let's go over that again: the SSEB scores each SSP standard according to your proposal's understanding of the problem, compliance with requirements, and soundness of approach.

Additionally, there may be General Criteria announced in the RFP Section M that the SSEB applies across all disciplines, such as Risk and (for Army proposals) MANPRINT. DoD uses three Risk categories—cost, schedule, and performance. FAA uses ten facets of risk—technical, operability, producibility, supportability, cost, schedule, programmatic, management, funding, and political

123

that you need to address for FAA proposals. The Army's MANPRINT emphasizes integration of seven domains —manpower, personnel, training, human factors, engineering, system safety, and health hazards that you need to address for Army proposals.

For our specific proposal, Section M also identified seven key "tenets" that the evaluators would look for in order to make a "best value" award. We included these in our Red Team instructions.

The SSEB presents its findings to the SSA, usually in color codes without identifying the specific offeror by name. The SSAC advises the SSA on other factors that might affect his/her decision, and the SSA makes the final decision. By the way: the SSA *almost always reads the Executive Summaries*!

Our Red Team Blueprint—That said, now we need to set up a structured Red Team Review that will (hopefully) ensure that the proposal makes it through the SSEB. You can see, from the above discussion, that simply handing your Red Team a copy of the RFP and your proposal may make you feel better, and might even improve your proposal, but has little value in significantly improving your win probability. This is how we set up the Red Team Review for the proposal mentioned at the start of this article.

1. We identified experts for each technical and management discipline germane to our proposal, and matched them in advance to specific proposal volumes and sections.

2. Every proposal section was reviewed by at least two reviewers, but no one had to review the entire proposal.

3. We set up the room the night before with tables, name plates with the individuals' functions noted, and reference materials.

4. We provided each member with a three-ring notebook with his/her name on the cover and the following material inside:

    a. Copy of the Red Team Review Plan and schedule

    b. List of all Red Team Members, their review assignments, and contact information

    c. List of proposal team management, volume leaders, authors, pubs people, and their contact information.

    d. Copy of the RFP Section L Instructions to Offerors (proposal organization instructions)

    e. Copy of RFP Section M Evaluation Factors for Award.

    f. Complete proposal Master Table of Contents (outline)

5. We provided copies of the proposal sections that each would be reviewing at their location

6. We provided copies of the RFP Shred-out to Proposal, showing the actual RFP Requirements that we were addressing in each numbered proposal paragraph (which had been "blessed" by the Pink Team much earlier)

7. We provided convenient copies of the complete RFP and reference documents for their use, if needed

8. We provided paper, Post-Its, paper clips, and red pens (no black pens or pencils allowed — too hard to see when the proposal pages are marked in black)

9. We provided stacks of Proposal Deficiency Reports (PDRs) with places to score: understanding of the problem, compliance with requirements, soundness of approach, and risk assessment and mitigation. All "yellow" and "red" scores required a PDR.

10. Because of the amount to be reviewed and the short time remaining before submittal, the reviewers were allowed to mark simple changes directly on the proposal draft with their red pens, placing a Post-It on the page so that we could find their markups easily.

The President/General Manager welcomed the Red Team, and after self-introductions all around, the Program Manager briefed the program, and I, as Red Team Leader, briefed the review process and Red Team Review Plan. And yes, we told them were to find coffee, donuts, and the bathrooms. We also provided lunch. All volume managers and authors attended this opening session so proposal team and Red Team would know each other, The authors were allowed to leave—even to go home since it was a weekend—but to stay within reach if the reviewers needed to contact them.

At the end of the first day, we held a Plenary Session to determine how the review was going. There have been times on other proposals when the Plenary brought to light the fact that the proposal draft was so rough and incomplete that it could not be reviewed. For that proposal, I reorganized the Red Team into a "Tiger Team," and assigned each member proposal sections to "Fix or Repair as Needed." This was the only way we got the proposal out (which, not surprisingly, lost anyway).

For this proposal, however, the review was going well, but, because of the complexities of the proposal and our offering, it was apparent that we would not be able to review the entire proposal as planned. Therefore, I split the team, reorganized the assignments and we were able to complete the review successfully the second day.

Automated Proposal Deficiency Reports—As the Red Team Reviewers completed proposal sections, they gave their completed PDRs to their panel leader who reviewed them, and then gave them to our Red Team Management group, where three of us entered the PDRs into the POW2000™ Red Team Review function. When we entered the PDRs, POW2000 automatically entered the reviewers' and author contact information, and the RFP Section M evaluation factor under which the proposal paragraph was evaluated. These PDRs could be organized and printed in order of Red Team Deficiency Control Number, proposal paragraph number, Red Team Panel, reviewer, or author. We printed and distributed hard copies, and e-mailed applicable copies to the volume leaders and authors, and to our teammates across the country.

Red Teams—time well-spent or a waste of time—This Red Team was very difficult, because of the short time to prepare the proposal and review materials, the complexities of the RFP and our proposal, the short time to review a large amount of material, and the short time to respond before submittal. We spent many 16-hour days preparing for it. The reason it worked, was because we planned and implemented a workable process, we provided everything the reviewers needed in a convenient format, and the volume managers, authors, pubs, and reviewers all cooperated.

For this Red Team Review, it was "Time Well Spent."

Table of Contents